T0197115

THE DIRTY-MINDED
CHRISTIAN

HOW TO

CLEAN UP

YOUR

THOUGHTS

WITH THE

ADAPT² Principle

KIRK THOMAS AND
LINDA THOMAS

THE DIRTY-MINDED CHRISTIAN
HOW TO CLEAN UP YOUR THOUGHTS
WITH THE ADAPT² PRINCIPLE

iUniverse books may be ordered through booksellers or by contacting:

iUniverse
1663 Liberty Drive
Bloomington, IN 47403
www.iuniverse.com
1-800-Authors (1-800-288-4677)

ISBN: 978-1-5320-2851-9 (sc)
ISBN: 978-1-5320-2853-3 (hc)
ISBN: 978-1-5320-2852-6 (e)

Library of Congress Control Number: 2017912968

Print information available on the last page.

iUniverse rev. date: 10/18/2017

Kirk's Dedication

This book is dedicated to my fellow ADAPT[2] colleague and partner in life, my wife Linda, and to my father, mother, and brother for their years of support, my son who keeps me young, and God who gives me strength. I also want to thank the volunteers and employees of the hundreds of pregnancy care centers I work with who unwittingly remind me of the value of possessing a servant's attitude.

Linda's Dedication

Writing a book has been a dream of mine and for making that and all my dreams come true, I thank my loving husband, Kirk. I offer special thanks to Jill McKellan, who has exhibited a tremendous amount of patience with both Kirk and me as we relied on her vast knowledge and skill in this process. To Lauren, Kaitlin, and Daniel, if God had told me I could choose any three children in the entire world, I'd have chosen each one of you. And lastly, thanks be to God for His guidance throughout this book and in all I do.

I dedicate this book to those who only see darkness and pray they discover the light that lives within us all.

CONTENTS

A MESSAGE TO ALL OF YOU WHO HAVE DIRTY MINDS

Writing a book to explain to others the profound impact a simple idea has made in our lives has not only been a big task, but one that has required a gigantic leap in faith. Yet, it was one we didn't hesitate to take on and since we began, it has been amazing to find out how much we've learned and grown as individuals and as a couple.

"With this book, I saw an opportunity to explain a simple concept that I developed, which has helped to create positive change in all areas of my life. My hope is that people who read this book can use it to improve the areas in their lives they may be struggling in. I've always been an avid reader, particularly with self-help/personal development books, finding that they contained lots of great information to pick and choose from for living a better life. What I also discovered was disconnection between understanding and knowing what you could do and being able to apply it to everyday life. Many times, it seemed too simple or too complicated, or the correct foundation for establishing the mindset wasn't in place. I've kept these things in mind as this book has been written. If you find that you possess a dirty mind, I am confident you can clean it up using the ADAPT^2 Principle because I can attest to how it has helped me clean up mine." ~Kirk Thomas~

"The purpose was originally to document something for Kirk and me to use. However, it quickly became a passion of both of ours to share it with others, hoping that it might positively impact their lives, too. Because of this experience, our marriage has grown stronger, our fitness has gotten back on track, our inner peace and confidence has grown, and our relationships have improved. Most importantly, my relationship with God has a new place, a permanent place within my heart." ~Linda Thomas~

INTRODUCTION

Do you have a dirty mind? I'm not asking if, while preparing hot dogs for your kids' lunch, you daydream about things like the steamy sex you and your spouse had in the shower earlier in the day. I'm talking about the kind of mind that allows negative thinking to prevail and screw up your life. Chances are you do. Of the approximately 50,000 thoughts researchers say we have during a 24-hour period, 80 percent of them are negative[1]. In other words, most folks do indeed have dirty minds.

The ADAPT[2] Principle is like a mop; it's there to help you clean up the filth between your ears. It's not a maid service, though. You can't hire someone to get inside your head and make you change the way you think. This is no more realistic than believing that simply telling yourself to "turn that frown upside down" will result in real change. Instead of living with an annoying message in your mind, why not abandon what does not work? Try the ADAPT[2] Principle. It will introduce you to a simple thought management process that is effective in cleaning out the dirt in all areas of your life for the rest of your life.

Oh, I know what your dirty little mind is telling you because I've also heard it a time or two. *Nothing can help me...I'm divorced... I'm terrible with money...I drink too much... I eat too many carbs... I stole candy from my kid's Easter basket... Blah, blah, blah, blah, blah!* Really, it doesn't matter how unworthy you think you are. There's hope for everyone. I'm not kidding!

Ever since Kirk and I met, we have shared everything, including the writing of this book and cleaning up our dirty minds. We have existed with dirty minds and are living proof about how this type of mind messes with us and loves the chaos it creates. So, if you're thinking that you're worse off than others, please know that you are not. We'd be glad to put our mistakes and sins up against any one of yours, any day! Be assured, we would only do so to demonstrate to you that you're not alone.

Through the ADAPT² Principle and God's grace, we have been able to develop a habit of using our thoughts to dream about and achieve things we previously thought (and believed) were meant only for other people. The word *adapt* literally means to make something suitable for a new use or purpose, which is exactly what ADAPT² does for us. By creating a shift in our thought patterns, we are offered the opportunity to revolutionize the way we think and react to everything from a brief encounter with a barista while ordering our morning cup of coffee to more serious issues with the people we love, and all with grace.

ADAPT² represents your *A-Attitude, D-Discipline, A-Action, P-Patience, T-Training,* and *T-Trust.* It's no secret that a positive attitude, self-discipline, follow-up through actions, maturity and self-control exhibited by patience, hard work and education through training, and trust in God is essential to sustained happiness and success in all aspects of our lives. It's through the simple and effective use of the acronym-a popular memory device-that we grow better able to think more effectively and efficiently. And in this case, we can focus on positive outcomes. This acronym is quite literally our mind's personal trainer.

Yes, we hear you. You're wondering how we know this will work for you. The answer: because it has worked for us and we are no different than anyone reading this book.

Each chapter is going to address all the dirt that piles up in life. It's not about sweeping it under the rug. It's about exposing it.

You're going to clean house with real life challenges and meaningful changes.

All the chapters will include:

- Stories from both Kirk's and my perspective. The $ADAPT^2$ Principle is of his creation, but I (Linda) am a practitioner of it as well as the main narrative voice throughout this book.
- Ways to extract what doesn't serve you well in your life so you can begin to focus on what will serve you better using the $ADAPT^2$ Principle.

Specifically, we are going to address the following:

1. How to make your A-Attitude one that is conducive to reaching your greatest potential in all areas of your life.
2. Ways to become more aware of your D-Discipline, recognizing when it is lacking and doing what is necessary to align it with what is good for the betterment of your life.
3. The art of A-Action, which is the foundation of everything you'll do. Nothing is achieved without meaningful action to create change. As wonderful as it would be, the sooner you accept things will not just happen without some effort the sooner you can begin to flourish in all capacities of your life.
4. The factor in the $ADAPT^2$ Principle in which many people struggle is P-Patience. Through some humor, grace, and a determination for something better, patience is born. We'll help you plant the seed to grow your patience.
5. Techniques to up your T-Training for what you wish to achieve in life. Creating solid relationships and showing self-love requires training, just as much as any other skill you'll ever learn or master.

6. The gold nugget in the Principle is T-Trust in God. This is the step that many discredit or don't focus on. It is a real difference maker. Trust in God makes the tough times easier and the amazing times better!

The six areas of your life where the ADAPT^2 Principle most often applies are:

1. Family
2. Social/Friends
3. Spiritual
4. Physical/Health
5. Work/Career
6. Financial

Our greatest wish is that what we share also provides you with some entertainment; at minimal, food for thought. This book is about two dirty-minded Christians with different backgrounds and experiences who strive every day to keep their minds clean with one life changing principle–the ADAPT^2 Principle.

The last chapter in this book is meant for starting your action to a positively driven mindset and way of doing more–often with less resistance. In this pivotal last chapter, we're going to get you started with the act of putting the principle into play through the power of two things:

- Developing a Personal Mission Statement
- Using an easy to follow worksheet to implement all parts of the ADAPT^2 Principle into your goals and specific purposes, which offers you a new, clean way to view life's events, take action, and create true balance and happiness in your life.

The worksheet is a useful guide that we both use and apply almost daily to help us better understand the meaningful changes in the six key areas of life that are its focus.

Are you ready to clean up your dirty mind and lead a more positively driven, principled life? We hope so. We can both assure you of one thing; since we've started doing this, we laugh more, we stress less, and we experience more out of everything and everyone in our day.

AND REMEMBER...

ADAPT² does not always present itself in a methodical manner such as A, D, A, P, T, T. There are times when you may take A-Action to adjust your A-Attitude so you can T-Trust that you are T-Training yourself with D-Discipline to keep you P-Patient in your pursuits. This combination and every other variation are possible. If you are mindful of keeping all six components of the principle in play, you will experience the difference. They are like a recipe. If one ingredient is missing, it may turn out okay, but it will not be as good as it possibly could have been. Kirk refers to this as the missing link–the gap that is in between you and really connecting with what you desire.

Will your mind always be a little dirty? Probably, because human nature dictates this. However, with the ADAPT² Principle you have the right tool to put a plan in place to clean it up quickly and achieve great things for your life.

So, roll up your sleeves and turn the page. It's time to do some cleaning!

CHAPTER 1

THE DIRTY ROAD

One of baseball legend Yogi Berra's most famous quotes is, "When you get to the fork in the road, take it." Some people say this was another one of his clever Yogi-isms, this time about decision making. In truth, Yogi has said he was simply giving Joe Garagiola directions to his home, which could be reached by taking either fork since they each merged at some point along the route.

Several years ago, Kirk had an idea. In deciding what to do with it, God put before him a fork in the road. Kirk chose to go the wrong way rather than the right way. While his journey along that path proved to be a bumpy one, it eventually led him to develop a life-changing concept. In many ways, it's like Robert Frost's poem, "The Road Not Taken," in which the message centers around taking the path that is worn and easier compared to that which fewer people travel, though those who do find wonderful rewards awaiting them at the end. And hey, if it's good enough for Yogi and a cool character like Mr. Frost, shouldn't it be good enough for us, too?

Kirk Confesses: I've Got a Dirty Mind

"Hello, my name is Kirk and I am an addict." Saying something so reprehensible about myself in front of dozens of strangers felt like an out of body experience. I recited what I felt needed to be said to

1

appease those who believed the confession to be true, but I really didn't think my gambling was a problem. After all, I was a highly successful commercial insurance broker. I paid my bills and had a wife, a son, parents, a brother, and friends who loved me. I wasn't like the addicts I'd seen on television or in the movies. In fact, most people thought I was rich in every way. But for me, it hadn't been enough.

So, what started out as an arrogant attempt to beat a game of chance that experts said was unbeatable turned into an obsession. For years I cycled through meaningless days spent in the underbelly of smoke-filled casinos pursuing an impossible dream. As each empty day passed I vowed never to return to the place I knew was draining me financially, emotionally, and spiritually. Yet, I failed.

A new day would dawn and there I'd be again, standing at a craps table with a bunch of pathetic souls. But not me. I believed I was different. I was smarter than everyone else. I knew when to walk away. If I lost my daily limit, so what? I'd simply chalk it up to a bad day. I just reasoned that by week's end I would be ahead of the game. I was the exception to the rule; no one else had the mind to figure it all out like I had.

Most right-minded people realize that in the long run a game of chance is an unbeatable foe, without exception. What they don't understand is that I really believed I had it figured out; you can win if, instead of focusing on the overwhelming chance you have of losing, you exploit the times when you have the lesser chance of winning. All I had to do was figure out when that time would come. And if anyone could do it, I could.

Hindsight paints a different picture. I now realize I had taken liberties with my positive attitude and used it in a very creative and destructive way.

Somehow losing was put in a convenient place; just another part of my business plan. After the loss was out of the way, it was time to move on to the goal of making sure I was prepared to win big when opportunity finally knocked. I began the painstaking process of learning everything I could to make that happen. I came across a statistics book that seemed familiar, perhaps I'd had a brief encounter with it back in high school. I had given it the cold shoulder back then, but embraced it now like I did my sweetheart during senior prom. I was mesmerized by the concepts within it. I restructured my *business* and made changing variables and deviations my partners. Ah, the glamorous life of a high roller.

I had discovered an important element to success at the craps table. But, figuring out the math was only half the battle. The real fight would take place in my own mind if I allowed it. I realized my thoughts would either make or break me. You see, it's easy for your mind to deceive you when your free time is spent losing more than just money in a casino. I had been living a secret life, which is a sad and lonely way to live. It resulted in my marriage ending, but that was not the only thing I lost. Hiding the truth from my friends about my extracurricular activities became too much of a chore, so I chose to alienate myself from them. But even *that* is not the worst of it. The toughest part was how I lost respect for myself. I would have prayed for God's help, but I felt as if I'd lost Him, too.

What to do? That became my pressing question. I was stuck at the bottom of this void and needed to find a way to climb out of it. Being smart enough, all things considered, I decided to use my mind to come up with a new plan. This plan would be one that would help me remain focused on my goal, regardless of my oppressive environment. Don't get me wrong, I didn't want to quit gambling, I just wanted to up the plan to a more logical one to prove I was right and everyone who doubted me was, well, wrong. I needed a simple plan, one that would allow me to adapt to the ever-changing conditions of the craps table and keep my thoughts and actions in check while I patiently waited for my time to come. *The word "adapt"; now that has possibilities for a winning plan*, I thought.

People in my inner circle began to voice their concern about my gambling and even threw out the word "addict." The word was not well received. You see, what they didn't know and would never understand was how I had experienced an epiphany of sorts; a manifestation of my mind's theory on how to beat the craps table. They just didn't get it or care to understand that I was like Bradley Cooper's character in the movie *Limitless*. Everything was clearer than it had ever been; only my drug wasn't NZT like in the film, it was the standard operating procedure I'd developed called the ADAPT Principle.

You might have noticed there was no second T to represent Trust in my original idea. At the time, it didn't occur to me how critical T-Trust in God is for any plan to succeed. Today, knowing that He would have a better use for my plan never ceases to inspire and amaze me!

You can't get rich, or be enriched when your office is a casino…

I was convinced my A-Attitude, D-Discipline, A-Action, P-Patience, and T-Training would propel me to new heights in the gambling world, an embarrassing ambition the way I see it today. But that was my misguided mindset then and I willingly abused the ADAPT Principle to make myself the King of the Casinos. I didn't acknowledge that eventually kings get knocked off their thrones or that there is only one true king and I wasn't Him.

NOTE: In case you're wondering, the ADAPT^2 Principle would come much later. The letters in the acronym are the same and what it represents is, too. It's just put to a much different use.

The *gambling* Kirk used ADAPT in this manner:

A-Attitude: The confidence that I would do what I set out to achieve ruled my attitude. I had to possess the right attitude to keep me in the game. Hell, I didn't even like playing craps. I just knew I'd figured the stupid game out and was there to prove it. I was unlike the regulars who were burdened with their own repressive negative attitudes. Unlike them, I knew being negative in any manner would be counterproductive and work against me. And if good things were happening to me, they were meant to be because I was focused on positive uses for my mind. That included gambling winnings when they came—and they most definitely would come.

D-Discipline: I developed the iron will to stick to my standard operating procedure. I committed myself to being mindful of the challenges I'd face along my quest and remained undeterred in reaching my goal. I would not linger around the craps table or in the casino after I won big. I wouldn't risk giving back what I so valiantly fought for to win.

A-Action: When I played craps, I'd imagine myself on a movie set. Of course, I was the film's star, waiting for the crew member holding a clapperboard to smack me into action at just the right time. At that moment, it was show time and I was ready, knowing that I had both the resources and confidence to take full advantage of a vulnerable craps table.

P-Patience: My patience was tried almost daily as I waited for my big win. If I wasn't patient and bet too much during the expected dry spell, my plan would fail and I wouldn't reach my goal. I couldn't make the dice, the table, or any of the other variables do something before it was meant to happen. So, there I sat, day after day, waiting patiently for my time to attack.

T-Training: Training your mind to perform under any circumstance can be difficult. For me, my training tool was a simple question: how do I ADAPT? To answer this question, I would run the letters of ADAPT and their meaning through my mind as I stood at the table. This was paramount to my success. I had to be physically and emotionally fit to make this work. My training allowed me to recognize when something good might happen. Clues were always present, and I knew how to hone in on them.

Eventually I began to reap what I had sown. I was winning at the craps table but losing at the game of life. This type of lifestyle was steadily taking a toll on my physical, mental, and emotional health. I had sunk to an all-time low and decided to look for solace one Sunday morning in a place I only occasionally visited. Prior to my gambling habit I had been a church-goer. But, getting up early to attend and missing out on sleep after a late Saturday night spent in a casino wasn't a sacrifice I had been willing to make in quite some time.

The message the pastor delivered that day was nothing short of divine intervention. He spoke about the crucifixion of Jesus; a story I had heard dozens of times before. As he detailed the events of Jesus' death, something about how the pastor retold the story this time made me sit up a little straighter. He seemed to be speaking only to me as he recounted the part when the Roman soldiers took Jesus' clothes and cast lots for them as he was tortured. My heart sank as I drew a parallel between the soldiers and myself. My head ached as only one thought was allowed in. *Oh, God. What am I doing?*

That night I awoke to a terrifying dream. I was at the base of the cross as Jesus was being crucified. I knelt, but not in reverence, far from it. I was one of the soldiers gambling for Jesus' clothing. My counterparts laughed as they found pleasure in their actions. I, on the other hand, looked up and met Jesus' eyes and only felt shame.

You might believe it was just a dream, but to me it was so much more. I will never forget the look I saw in Jesus' eyes. It was then that I vowed to commit the rest of my life for His purpose, not for my own. And it was then that I truly started to live!

**What good is it for someone to gain the whole
world, yet forfeit their own soul?**
(Mark 8:36, NIV)

God has blessed each one of us with the abilities to become productive members of society. I wasn't a bad person; however, in looking back, I realize I had not used my talents in the way they were intended to be used.

The ADAPT Principle had proven to be a useful tool for organizing my thoughts at the craps table. I saw no reason why it couldn't be put to better use in other areas of my life such as in my physical, financial, and emotional fitness. I continued to ask, "How do I ADAPT?" This was my source of guidance and it lead me toward successful results.

From this time on, I gained peace of mind, as I knew that the ADAPT Principle ensured me of doing what was within my power to cope with changing situations in the most optimal way possible.

Still, I knew there was something missing, although I didn't know what exactly.

At this point, I had long since been divorced. My career was going well, though, and I had regained the physical fitness that suffered from years spent in the toxic environment of a casino. Things were looking up... and then I met Linda. Ah, this is what had been missing!

Linda Confesses: I've Got a Dirty Mind

I met Kirk in God's perfect time. It had been about six years since I had gone through an incredibly ugly divorce following a 25-year marriage. Those years were the most difficult of my life. I was sick and tired of being sick and tired. I guess you could say I had reached my own fork in the road. The way I saw it, I could continue down a very dark path and remain in my depressed state. Or, I could retake control and just be happy. Nothing had changed other than my resolve. I looked brave, but I was truly scared. I knew I wasn't equipped to sustain the optimism I felt in those defining moments. It was a temporary fix to get me through a period, but hardly enough to get me through my life.

Previously, I had already made several futile attempts to change my hopeless attitude, but the negative circumstances of my life and the focus I gave them always seemed to bring me down. I desperately wanted to reach my destination; to be happy regardless of those many things I couldn't control, but feared I would be the car that hits empty just short of the gas station.

After meeting Kirk, it didn't take long for us to feel comfortable enough with each other to begin sharing intimate details of our lives. During one of these private conversations he told me about the ADAPT Principle, how it originated, and how it ultimately turned into the catalyst for the real change he needed.

It was obvious and amazing. Together we recognized God's presence in our journey. Without our faith in Him, we knew nothing was possible, but through Him the possibilities were and are endless. So, we added a second T and vowed to place our T-Trust in God and at that moment the ADAPT² Principle was born. It's amazing how God took a destructive, self-centered thought and transformed it into a guiding light that provided hope and prosperity for both of us.

I became an unwitting student of the ADAPT² Principle. At first, I accepted parts of it, but rejected others. For example, I refused to complete the Personal Mission Statement Worksheet, thinking it was a waste of my time. I reasoned that I hadn't followed through with goals I'd set before and this would be no different. But, it was clear what I had done in the past hadn't worked well for me. Perhaps, I did need to get with the program for sustainable change to take place. It was only when I disciplined myself and did the work that I realized the full benefit of a clean mind.

Once I opened my mind, it became easy to remember what each of the letters in ADAPT² represented. My new challenge was to fully grasp the role of each element when it came to how they fit together–and worked together. I began to think of them as a family. Everyone in a family is important and can succeed as an individual. But, when members lean on and support one another, life is even better. Before long, this little family established residency in my mind and has been happily living there ever since!

Our Message to You: Be Fearless and Live Your Life

Are you afraid of what your future holds? Maybe you're so caught up in just making it through the day that you've lost sight of what you want for your life. Or, is it that you've never even made the time to figure out what you want your life to look like? You live like a ping-pong ball being batted back and forth with no control over which side of the table you end up on?

Whether you have money troubles, weight issues, relationship or work-related problems, there's no better time than now to empower yourself to be happy–despite them. It's time to visualize your dreams and commit to using the ADAPT² Principle to develop the habits necessary to live your life to its fullest potential. You don't need to be afraid, because we are going to help.

Here's some additional great news: you don't need extra time in your day to develop the ADAPT² lifestyle. In fact, you will save precious time by not wasting it on non-productive, thoughts and activities. Your time will be spent on reaching the goals you've determined are important to you to be successful in all areas of your life.

This journey will take you from speculation to A-Action as you go through each chapter of the book. An area that you'll want to be particularly mindful of is the last chapter about creating a Personal

Mission Statement. Your statement is your positive, motivating guide– eliminating fear and giving your drive a purpose.

You stick with us, we'll stick with you, and before long you'll be asking yourself, "How do I ADAPT[2] this situation?" And you'll know just how to figure it out!

CHAPTER 2

ADAPT²: THE IMPACT OF A DIRTY A-ATTITUDE

My stepfather, Leo, was a man who demonstrated a positive attitude throughout his life. As a young woman, it always intrigued me. The greatest example of this was in how he handled his own death. Leo was diagnosed with Alzheimer's disease at the age of 87. I remember having lunch with him soon after our family was dealt the frightening news. He expressed confusion about what was happening to his mind, but never complained or asked, "Why me?" For the next three years, we watched the disease slowly destroy his brain. Even in this altered state, Leo seemed to refuse to allow the horrible disease to wreck his A-Attitude. Days after we celebrated Leo's 90th birthday, he died. Just hours before Leo's beautiful heart beat for the last time the doctor entered his room and asked, "Leo, how are you doing today?" With closed eyes and through shallow breath, he whispered, "I can't complain."

Whether Leo came by his amazing strength in attitude naturally or it was something he had to work at to develop really doesn't matter. It was the most endearing attribute he possessed. You could say, it was everything.

11

Grade A-Attitude

"Attitude is everything" is possibly the most re-quoted motivational expression of our time. It's often presented as a statement of fact since few would argue against the importance of a positive one.

But, what exactly is attitude and why is it so darn important? Attitude is your interpretation of the world and the way you think and react within it. Simply put, it's the difference between being happy in life and merely existing.

A proper attitude is so crucial and wonderfully demonstrated through the way the Apostle Paul addresses it in his Letter to the Ephesians. He wrote:

You were taught, with regard to your former way of life, to put off your old self, which is being corrupted by its deceitful desires to be made new in the attitude of your minds.
(Eph. 4: 22-24, NIV)

Because of the significance of one's attitude, it is not by coincidence that the first letter in ADAPT[2] stands for *attitude*. A positive mental approach to your life is the be-all and end-all of the ADAPT[2] Principle. It's the ice cream in your sundae. Without it, nothing else makes sense. Without a healthy mental attitude, your quality of life suffers. My stepfather, Leo, certainly had his share of struggles, but chose to be happy despite them. Please understand, I am not suggesting that possessing a positive attitude is as easy as making up your mind to have one. Like any worthwhile cause, remaining positive oftentimes takes effort and unshakeable faith.

Science has proven that for some, thinking happy thoughts may be more difficult than for others. According to a Michigan State Study[1] published in *The Journal of Abnormal Psychology*, there are negative and positive people in the world who literally are born this way. Fortunately, that doesn't mean these people can't learn to see the glass half full instead of half empty. It might just be more of a challenge for them. Just remember, ADAPT^2 is for anyone who has a burning desire to adopt good habits for a better A-Attitude regardless of their genetic make-up.

Do You See the Donut or the Hole?

It's impossible to be truly happy with a bad attitude. Think about it… Do any of you know a happy person with a negative attitude? I don't. I know plenty of folks who pretend to be happy, but reveal the truth they desperately try to hide or deny by exposing harsh words and deeds. We cannot behave in a way that is inconsistent with our thinking for any length of time. In other words, our attitude will both precede and determine the quality of our emotional state. The good news is we have the power within ourselves to reframe any situation and our reaction to it. The ADAPT^2 Principle was designed as a system to help people do just that in their daily lives. Remember, it's a thought shift process.

Here's a lighthearted little prayer for you to remember in those times where you are attitude challenged:

A Prayer to Encourage a Fun Attitude

God, give me sympathy and common sense,
And help me home with courage high.
God, give me calm and confidence
And please—a twinkle in my eye.

Do the people you encounter see the twinkle in your eye?

Don't Believe Everything You Think

Let's start by identifying what your first thoughts tend to be. Are they typically negative or positive? Be honest with yourself. There is no point in being any different. There are no wrong or right answers. This exercise in identifying your thoughts is meant to provide you with a baseline as to how to proceed in further contemplation on your current habits. The following examples might help you determine your tendencies:

- Let's say you put on a new outfit and your boyfriend gushes, "Wow! You look hot in that dress. You look ten pounds thinner in it." Is your first thought, "OMG! He just called me fat!" Or, are you more likely to assume he is truly paying you a compliment?
- What if your boss says, "There are going to be some changes around here." Do you assume something bad is coming down the pike? Even if you are the top dog in the workplace, do you first entertain the idea you might be fired rather than promoted?
- Do you convince yourself you have breast cancer when your doctor simply suggests you get a mammogram every year instead of every other year due to your family's history of it, or are you grateful you have a health care professional who provides service beyond anything generations before you had?

So, were you able to identify the kind of attitude you typically take? Truthfully, I suspect I might be one of those people born with a brain wired for negative thoughts and some friends may have given subtle suggestions–Linda, don't assume the worst, okay?

Using the above scenarios in the past, I most likely would have assumed my boyfriend had just insulted me or that I should probably update my resume because my boss was about to drop the hammer on me. However, since adopting the ADAPT[2] lifestyle, I've gained confidence in my ability to steer my negative perspective toward a more positive one and am much happier because of it. I no longer make mountains out of mole hills.

ADAPT[2] challenges you to learn to re-interpret the events of your life. It invites you to make a conscious decision to assess every situation you find yourself in and check your A-Attitude against the possibilities of it until seeing the most positive scenario becomes second nature.

Start by asking yourself: am I recognizing the positive as well as the negative? Which one has my focus? Acknowledging this is crucial because our first thoughts or interpretations are not always the correct ones, which means we must examine other possibilities. Your reaction to your wrong interpretation of events can be embarrassing at best or disastrous at worst.

Imagine this:

You walk into a room and find your husband on Facebook. He's so mesmerized by something he doesn't notice you at first. When he does see you he quickly closes his laptop and smiles at you. What is truly a genuine smile is suspicious to you.

"What's going on?" you wonder out loud as you feign cheeriness. What you'd really like to do is reach out and grab his laptop from him and confront him with the truth you know is hidden inside.

"Nothing," he says. You interpret his innocent response as one that warrants suspicion. He's hiding something, you suspect.

You say, "Fine." However, it is in that special way you reserve for your husband to let him know things are anything but "fine."

The air in your home becomes noticeably thicker with tension. You can feel the anger in your attitude heating up and you seize the opportunity to check his laptop for proof of his guilt about something. You feel the stress and anxiety build in your gut as you hurriedly pull up his Facebook page and scroll through the *likes* regarding a comment he recently made.

You recognize every one of his Facebook friends who *liked* the post except one—a very attractive young blond woman. "I knew it," you grumble to yourself. At that moment, your husband walks in the room and busts you by asking you the same question you had asked him earlier. "What's going on?" He seems mad, which makes you even madder. You turn the screen toward him so he can see the incriminating evidence you found. You justify your snooping and admit your suspicion about the blond woman who dared to *like* one of your husband's FB comments.

He gently takes the laptop from you and, without a word, clicks on her name bringing up her profile page. It is at that moment that you feel a sense of shame and relief all at once. She's a party planner; one, he goes on to explain, that he just hired to consult with for your upcoming wedding anniversary.

Oops! You did it again. This isn't the first time you jumped to the wrong conclusion about the man you vowed to love, honor, and respect. You know if you don't stop this destructive behavior you'll push your husband away and there won't be another anniversary to celebrate.

And why? Because your A-Attitude was driven by the jealousy monster instead of an *A-Awesome* attitude about your spouse.

You see, whether you were wired for negativity at birth or have formed negative thought habits over the course of your life, chronic *stinking thinking* is a happiness stealer that can and will do real damage. The positive in this scenario is that you can train your mind to identify and consider the possible good in any situation. Thankfully, you can adapt your A-Attitude and let go of the negativity of your assumptions.

Kirk Says, "It's Just Mud!"

Even before I could spell the word motorcycle, I was passionate about riding one. In fact, I raced motorcycles as a six-year-old and continued in the sport until I was a young adult. I loved it! In fact, I raced motocross throughout the United States and was consistently one of the top amateur racers in the nation. I even turned pro for a short time. Anyway, traveling and competing in a sport I lived and breathed provided me with innumerable opportunities to meet some wonderful people and experience amazing things.

However, there were downfalls to being a motocross racer, too; the high risk of injury inherently involved in the sport was something I needed to prepare for every day. To minimize the physical risk, I wore protective gear. Items such as boots, a helmet, and racing goggles were required pieces of equipment. Goggles were one of the most essential items as I relied on them to shield my eyes from the dirt, mud, and debris that constantly flew-up and assaulted me during practice or a race.

Through those goggles it's easy to demonstrate how I started using the ADAPT^2 Principle in my everyday life down the road, long past my racing days. You see, I absolutely needed those goggles to see where I was going and navigate the race course. During a thirty-minute race, mud and dirt constantly flew up toward my face, stopping and accumulating on my goggles and clouding my vision.

As the race continued, mud would keep piling up—more and more—until my vision was completely blocked and I couldn't see where I was going. During the race, I didn't have time to stop and physically clean my goggles. The solution was tear-offs.

Tear-offs are formed pieces of plastic with a pull-off tab that is in the same shape as the goggles. Before a race would begin, I would mount several tear-offs over my goggles. Then, when my vision would become impaired during the race, I could just reach up and pull one of the tabs. The tear-off would fly off and I instantly had clear vision once again.

How does all this relate to the ADAPT^2 Principle?

Think about all the mud that life throws at you every single day, impacting your attitude as a result. If you are out there living, you're going to encounter it. Maybe you wake up late on Monday morning and start off your entire week behind schedule. On a day when you can least afford it, traffic is extra heavy on your way to work, making you late. One afternoon, you find out you don't get a sale that you were counting on. Your boss reprimands you for missing an important deadline. One of your kids is doing poorly in school. The problems seem endless, but the real kicker is when you have an unexpected, very expensive car repair that you can only pay for by dipping into the money you were saving for a much-needed vacation.

All these challenges add up and block your vision–you feel emotionally stunted and quite overwhelmed. What's going on? You can't tell because your vision is so clouded. I have learned to use the ADAPT[2] Principle just like one of those tear-offs. Whenever I recognize my vision becoming distorted from life's challenges, I tap into the ADAPT[2] Principle and pull the tab. There is an instant sense of peace, and clarity is gained as a result, making my A-Attitude immediately better.

Visualize pulling your own tear-off when life throws mud your way. Imagine the mud being cleared from your eyes. Now you can see where you are going once again. No more bogged down feelings exist, because you are mentally and emotionally removing the mud that's blocking your vision, which in return impacts your attitude. When

I first conceptualized the ADAPT² Principle, I didn't even consider how it could work for this, but through the years I have discovered it does. Now when I am faced with one of life's challenges or adversities I simply tell myself, "It's just mud," and allow the ADAPT² Principle to take over and quickly clear my vision and improve my attitude.

What mud do you have in your life? Do you allow it to block your vision?

Is your dirty mind giving you an equally dirty attitude?

It's time to ADAPT² it!

At Times It's Easy to be Stubborn about Mud

I used to date a girl that worked in the sales department at a radio station. Let's just call her Linda. Hint, hint! Anyway, she stumbled into an awkward situation where she happened to be in the office when a call from a potential advertiser came in. Linda did all the right things, including asking the caller if they had been working with another rep from the station. They said they had not so, Linda did the work and made the sale. Great news, right? Wrong.

Linda called me and I could hear how upset she was. I asked her what was wrong and she explained her frustration at working hard and being rewarded with a big fat donut-zilch. Company policy was for the account holder to earn the commission, regardless of the circumstances of the sale. My response didn't sit well with her in the moment as I quipped, "It's just mud." If we had been in the same room at the time, I seriously think she would have thrown more than mud at me!

My timing could have been better, but what she really wanted to do was to express her anger more than anything else, which was fine. We all need to do this sometimes. Still, I tried to help her "pull the tear-off" so she could clearly see the possible solutions to what seemed to be an unfair situation. "Can't you go to your boss or the sales rep to discuss getting at least half of the commission?" I asked.

"No," she groaned.

Then I suggested that perhaps she could work with one of her co-worker's other clients in the future for a full commission and treat it like an account trade. I was relieved when she perked up and said, "Yes, that could happen."

"Then it's just mud," I said.

Linda knew all along that an account adjustment might be an option, but was too caught up in her negative emotions to see it as a possible solution. Once the mud was cleared, the answer to her problem became obvious.

On a side note: Sometimes the people you are close to come to you with their problems and expect you to vent right alongside them. But, are you really helping them when you do that? The next time a friend or family member comes to you and is frustrated by a problem they would rather complain about than find a solution for, remind them that "it's just mud" and help them pull their tear-off.

Linda Says, "That's Enough Talking, Mr. Ed!"

There are a few things you need to be aware of on your journey to developing a positive approach in handling life events through the ADAPT^2 Principle. For one, there will be people you know who like the rut they're stuck in. Furthermore, they prefer you stay in the rut with them rather than either of you getting out. It's the epitome of misery loves company. Let me introduce you to someone who used to be my friend. His name is Ed.

A few years after my divorce, my three children and I moved into what my ex-husband contemptuously referred to as a "renovated garage." In truth, it was an old carriage house with a certain amount of charm. Still, it was a far cry from the dream home we had lived in. It had been a swift and abrupt process to go from a beautiful house to that place, but it was my only reasonable option, as I had been a stay-at-home mom most of my married life. Now I was primarily responsible financially for my kids and me, which included keeping a roof over our heads.

After about a year, I landed a job which afforded me the opportunity to move from the carriage house to a luxury apartment in a desirable community. I invited a friend over to see it shortly after moving in. I felt a sense of pride as I gave Ed the quick tour. He knew about many of my struggles and marveled at my recent accomplishments. He complimented me on how I had decorated the place and said it could be featured in a magazine. I was on top of the world! Then, in the same breath as he congratulated and encouraged me, he warned, "Enjoy it now, Linda. You know it won't last." Wow! He rained on my parade just as I'd positioned my float at the start line! I replied, "You know, Ed, you might be right; but, I sure don't want to think about the lows during one of my highs."

Are there any Eds in your world? Do any of your friends or family members fixate on the negative? How do you respond? Like nasty little viruses, poor attitudes are contagious. Make sure you're vaccinated against them. Recognize problems, and then quickly move forward by focusing on positive solutions for them.

The "Inadequate" Attitude: Linda's Heavy Heart

In 2004, I made an appointment with my family doctor about a sore throat. No one was more surprised than me when I blurted out to him, "I'm depressed." Intense, negative feelings had been festering inside me for years, eating away at my happiness and my self-worth. Before that moment, I'd been unable to muster up the courage to speak those two words, which were profoundly hard to admit.

My doctor was calm and direct. "Well, if you think you are depressed, you probably are." Then he went on to explain three options for potential treatments, which were to talk with a professional therapist, take medication, or do a combination of the two. I'll admit, I did not like the choices, especially the potential stigma I perceived as a side effect of being on antidepressants. So, I opted for therapy, hoping it would be enough for me to get over the hump and onto living.

A few days later I found myself seated in front of a white-haired lady with old-fashioned, black rimmed glasses that made her look years older than I suspected she was. Somehow, I gained instant comfort in an office that was as unadorned as she was. She asked a couple questions—starter questions perhaps—and I found myself beginning to spew out what I'd been choking back for more than two decades. It all stemmed from a single harsh reality: I was angry at my husband. After two, one-hour sessions the journey to my depression was explained. It seems that I had turned that anger inward, causing my depression as a result.

It was decided that the best solution would be to go to marriage counseling. Reluctantly, my husband agreed. However, after a couple of attempts at it, my husband told me that he felt under attack from the counselor and her questions. He would no longer attend.

The news made me feel helpless and hopeless once again, resulting in a resolve to live unhappily in a loveless marriage. In 2008, I went back to the same therapist, hoping to get some help again to fight the depression that never left, but often crept into the forefront of my mind. At the end of our first session she took out the notes she'd kept in my file from 2004 and read them to me. The conclusion, everything I had said to her four years prior, I had just repeated. Nothing had changed. I was still depressed, struggling to fake it through the day for the sake of my three children and my own pride.

Shortly after, I told my husband our marriage was over.

After what felt like one of the most destructive divorces in history—to me, my husband, and our children—our marriage was finally legally over two years later. I was once again single. The last time I claimed that status I was twenty-one and childless. That was the old me, not the current me that was unprepared for a new world of singleness in which I knew nothing about.

Then I experienced something full force. I'd seen it in others before, but never dreamed I'd go through it. I refer to as the *divorce crazies*. I behaved like someone I did not recognize, finding myself looking at a stranger in the mirror more than myself. And, I loathed this stranger.

As much as I loved being my kids' mother, my break-up created a big identity struggle for me. I just didn't know who I was any longer. My kids were so upset by my transformation they would cry, "We just want our mother back!" And I wanted to be there for them more than I could explain. Still, hindsight shows that I wasn't really present at those moments when they needed me most.

After being a stay-at-home mom for so long, I was now a single woman in my forties. It was time to start a new game of life. I decided to go back into a career in broadcast advertising; one I had left when I went on maternity leave more than a decade earlier. It was necessary for my survival, as well as a way to address some serious financial concerns that began prior to the divorce and were only made worse throughout it. What did this mean? It meant that the responsibility fell squarely on my shoulders to keep me and my kids afloat financially and emotionally.

I can't imagine ever being more stressed out than I was during those years. If the divorce process was a battle between me and my soon to be ex-husband, the years following was a war I'd waged upon myself. Sadly, my children were the collateral damage. I was barely able to take care of myself, much less three innocent kids. I made horrible decision after horrible decision in relationships and other areas of my life.

The stress was so bad I could literally feel and see my heart pounding through my chest. The small amount of food I could choke down went right through me because my stomach was always in knots. Bad self-care and actions became abundant. I lost a ton of weight in a short amount of time. I began relying on the numbing effects of alcohol to lull me to sleep at night (a big change for someone who'd barely drank before). It all piled up. I was at a juncture in my life where I needed to make as much money as possible, but my lifestyle and mindset was making it increasingly difficult even to get out of bed to start my day. I was short-tempered and abrasive at times, too. Really, I hated myself for the negativity breeding inside of me, but I didn't know how to control it. I trusted no one, not even God.

Then there were my children—the innocents. They were suffering the sins of their parents and the guilt was crippling for me, truly unbearable. I began thinking horrible thoughts such as they would be better off without me. I rationalized that if I committed suicide, they would be able to share my life insurance and not have to suffer financially. It wasn't that simple, though, because for them to cash in I would have to make it look like an accident. I'd imagine myself driving into the barrier that separated the eastbound lanes of the highway from the westbound lanes. A few times I even closed my tear-filled eyes only to jerk them open after a couple seconds, fearing I'd crash into and hurt someone else instead of only myself.

It was such a downward spiral, with no hope of a positive outcome in sight. I just wanted to surrender.

But thankfully I did not. A couple months later, I met Kirk. He was cute, funny, charming, successful in his sales career, and in great physical shape. He was also one of the most positive people I'd ever met. Whenever I asked him how his day was going he would flash his toothy smile and say, "Great, as usual!" What a refreshing attitude!

I discovered Kirk was an avid self-help book reader. He believed in the messages of many, but recognized a need for a resource to help readers like him sustain lessons quickly forgotten. Critics of self-help often site short-term results as a problem of the genre, but this type of book has proven itself to be inspirational for long-term positive life changes in Kirk's life, and now mine, as well.

Kirk had so much information to share, and in such a positive manner, that I was drawn to it like a sponge. He shared the acronym he'd created with me, and told me how he'd used it to help him through some very tough times. Then he shared how he uses it every day because there are certain lessons that he never wanted to lose sight of again.

I was interested, but admittedly skeptical. However, I was driven by the fear of going back to my negative way of thinking. So, I gave it a try and committed to becoming more familiar with the ADAPT^2 way of life.

Together, Kirk and I began forming this wonderful team as we both learned to navigate our way through situations which had previously seemed overwhelming. We believed in the importance of positivity long before ADAPT^2. But, the ADAPT^2 Principle provided us with a tool we could use daily to stay positive in any given circumstance.

One area of our lives in which we have gained great benefit from the principle is about being mindful regarding our ex-spouses. I'd spent too much time dealing in negative thoughts about mine, but after I began to use the ADAPT^2 Principle it enabled me to focus on my three children, which wouldn't be in my life if my ex-husband hadn't been in mine. Both of us made a pact to have only one thought when it came to our ex-spouses no matter what the challenge with them might be. *Our exes helped us create our beautiful children.* Now we make it a point to always refer to that one positive thought whenever the need arises. Steps like this make the difference in addressing a negative thought right away. We have enabled ourselves to move on to the good and circumvent this type of negativity all together.

Once I started applying ADAPT^2 to all areas of my life, it grew into a habit for good. I stopped focusing on the *what ifs*. Now I take the A-Attitude that everything throughout my life has led me in perfect timing to this very moment. Honestly, I feel blessed for every experience, good and bad, in my life. Without the hurt, anger, disappointment, and heartache, I couldn't possibly feel the depth of gratitude, joy, excitement, and happiness I feel today.

My mind is cleaner now and there is a light that illuminates from within it, offering strength and optimism in lieu of all that dirty stuff.

Baggage is Meant for Vacations

Before I met Kirk, I allowed a man I was in a serious relationship with steal what little positivity and hope I had at the time. We'd been together for more than a year when he said to me, "If I had known you had all this baggage, I would never have gotten involved with you." Literally ripping my heart out couldn't have felt much worse. I don't remember how I reacted specifically, but have never forgotten how worthless those cold, harsh words made me feel.

During that period of my life, I wasn't in the habit of looking for the positive in things. If I had been, I would have realized the blessing he'd given me by spewing those cruel words. Truthfully, he had simply revealed himself to me in a profound way. He was not someone who would ever be the kind of loving man I needed and deserved in my life. I stayed in that destructive relationship for several more months despite what he'd said. My self-worth was so low at that time, I reasoned it was better to be happy during the 20 percent of the time I could trick myself into thinking things were good with him, than to be unhappy 100 percent of the time without him. Talk about stinking thinking!

As I became increasingly frustrated with his lying, cheating, and drinking, he became increasingly frustrated with me for voicing my negative opinions about his behavior. So, it was inevitable that we eventually broke up.

It didn't take me very long to start to feel better, even thankful about the breakup. Still, my ex's words had left an ugly scar. I felt like I was damaged goods, not worthy of being loved. As I mentioned earlier, that changed after I met Kirk.

Early in our relationship I shared with Kirk what I viewed as the atrocities of my past. I remember him trying to convince me I was no different than anyone else; that we all have baggage. Determined to remain stuck in my negative opinion of myself, I argued that my baggage was much worse than anyone else's. Undeterred, Kirk stated his case, a most compelling insight. "Linda, maybe you just need someone to help you unpack it."

He said it and I resisted it for a bit, but I could not forget his words. He offered to be there and he was a good and kind man. His willingness to help wasn't something he *had* to do. It was something he *wanted* to do. Wow! Finally, I allowed myself the gift of belief and I did believe that Kirk meant what he offered. Now the only baggage we keep around our happy home is for vacations!

Is there baggage you carry around in your mind that needs to be unpacked? Do you know someone who hangs on to their baggage? Instead of piling more on, how can you help them unpack it?

Make Self-Talk Your BFF

The people you allow in your life certainly have a major impact on your attitude, so choose them wisely. Perhaps the most intrusive obstacle you'll encounter; however, is yourself. Your inner voice can be your best friend or your worst enemy. Too often our own negative self-talk results in a hypercritical evaluation about our self to our self. Oftentimes, we aren't even aware of this destructive behavior and we passively allow negative thinking to intrude on our thoughts and make them our reality as a result.

No one is immune from the obstacles created with negative self-talk. They are a hindrance from everyone from the high performing athlete to the stay at home parent. The behaviors and habits which stem from this impact both personal and professional relationships, as well as the happiness factor of your life.

A great way to better grasp the vital importance of self-talk is to use this analogy:

Think about your home and everything in it. How would you protect it from a criminal? What security measures would you take? You would probably keep the lights on outside at night when criminal activity is most likely to occur. Obviously, you would lock the doors and windows to keep the bad guys out. Maybe you would get a dog. Perhaps you would even install a security system.

Like a security system for your home, an internally wired, faith-driven security system is essential to protect you from dirty self-talk, because too often your inner voice prohibits you from making the most of who you truly are—a beautiful child of God.

Using awareness, new habits can offer the solutions you need to create stronger positive connections in your thought patterns. This is a great way to improve your A-Attitude.

Fix your thoughts on what is true and good and right.
Think about things that are pure and lovely, and
dwell on the fine, good things in others. Think about
all you can praise God for and be glad about.
(Philippians 4:8 TLB)

The Mind Fueled by Positivity

From the example above, now imagine your mind as your home and your positive attitude as the most valuable possession in it. Your negative self-talk is the thief who targets the minds that are easiest to penetrate. There's something powerful about negativity that attracts these thieves just like you had an open door there that said, "Welcome. Come on in and invade me." Negativity is attracted to negativity. You'd never do this willingly or knowingly, of course, which is important to understand.

But what about A-Action?

Just as you would take efforts to develop a plan for your home's security, you must also do the same for your positive attitude. Guard it with all you have. After all, few things are as valuable to your mental well-being.

Turn your mind's light on so you can see the self-talk thief approach. Ask yourself, "How do I ADAPT[2] to this intruder?"

Lock the doors and windows of your mind to keep negative self-talk out.

When the negative self-talk thief surprises you and gains entry inside your mind's door, immediately sound the alarm and stop the thief in its tracks!

Do you remember Stuart Smalley? Stuart Smalley was a character created by Saturday Night Live writer, Al Franken, who introduced himself to the show's viewers in February of 1991. Through Smalley, Franken used satire to draw attention to our culture's over-the-top obsession with an individual's self-worth and the importance of using daily affirmations, or positive self-talk, to inflate it. While Smalley's motto, "I'm good enough, I'm smart enough, and doggone it, people like me," is intentionally silly, the bottom line is not. Positive self-talk is crucial to possessing the right attitude. Likewise, affirmations can be helpful for some people.

Affirmations keep those who give credence to them better motivated and focused on goals. They are tools for tweaking our subconscious mind into changing the way we think, as well as promoting feelings of positivity, energy, and activity. Unfortunately, most of us find it much easier to say something nice to people we barely know than to ourselves.

I've never had trouble whipping out compliments to complete strangers I only have brief encounters with. It makes me feel good to make someone else feel good. Are you that same way? If you are, it creates a pressing question: why is it so hard, even uncomfortable, for so many of us to treat ourselves in the same kind way?

You could have asked me that for many years and received nothing more than a blank stare back, or perhaps a weak justification of some type. This was because I had no idea why I couldn't treat myself as well as I treated others, until I began following the ADAPT[2] Principle. Only then did I begin creating a habit to use positive self-talk to clean out all that dirty self-talk that had made itself at home in my mind.

If you embrace perfection, or on the opposite end of the scale fear rejection, you beat yourself up constantly. You either expect nothing or too much, both of which are equally detrimental.

Imagine how the value you assign yourself would skyrocket if you made it a habit to replace every negative thought about yourself with a positive one. I'd bet the farm on that stock tip! Breaking a habit of self-deprecation and replacing it with self-affirming thoughts isn't easy and won't happen overnight. However, it is critical to cleaning up your dirty mind.

But, Did You Know this about Creating Habits?

They say that it takes only twenty-one days to develop a habit. This is true for some, but be kind and loving to yourself by knowing that this is not true for everyone. Why is this important? It's important because we should lift ourselves up for success, not failure. More than the number of days it takes to create a habit, achieving a focus on at least improving a bit each day is something of great value. A-Action is required, as thoughts alone are not enough.

Consider this scenario:

A person who has been weighted down with negativity his or her entire life, living and growing up in an environment where the positive was never accentuated. Negative thoughts have become a part of their very fabric, a state of being that is the only one familiar to them. Compare this individual to someone who has usually been positive and has experienced personal fulfillment or success on some level, but then something goes wrong that jars them. They struggle and resist what's happening, finding themselves growing exhausted, and feeling quite negative about everything—all a result of that small handful of things.

The person who has experienced positivity may only need those twenty-one days to rebound back to where they were with new habits. However, the person who has had a lifelong struggle will likely need more time, but every day with an effort to positively affirm their life is an unmistakable day of progress.

Don't tie yourself down to other's expectations for your progress because that may leave you feeling like a failure (even when you are not). Commit to your own hopes and aspirations for success, acknowledging the goodness in taking a small step forward every day. Remember the power of the tortoise's actions in the classic children's fable, "The Tortoise and the Hare?" Just because you can move fast doesn't mean you are doing things right, or that you are more focused. Also remember, you are going to have negative thoughts if you're wired that way, and it truly comes down to the power that you allow them to have over your actions and self-perceptions that ultimately matters.

Habit creation on your time and not some stated time is nothing new to us in writing this book. In a 2009 University College London[2] study, researchers examined the new habits of ninety-six individuals over a span of twelve weeks. What they found that is significant to us is: the average time required for someone to create a new habit was sixty-six days. Additionally, individual times varied from eighteen to a whopping 254 days! Another interesting perspective that this study found was that breaking a habit and creating a habit are usually different sides of the same coin, meaning that some of the worst habits we create for ourselves can take that amount of time to develop, as well. By keeping this in mind, you can really give yourself grace, compassion, and understanding for your life's journey, which is so essential.

Trivia question: Do you know where the twenty-one days guideline came from? The answer is by plastic surgeon Maxwell

Maltz, who wrote a book called *Psycho Cybernetics* in 1960 and used that number referring to patients who seemed to take about twenty-one days to get used to their new faces. Strange how twenty-one days for that purpose has worked its way to such a perceived fact in today's world.

Attitude Preparation Versus Attitude Reaction

Kirk has been able to compellingly share insight on attitude through using the ADAPT[2] Principle. He firmly believes anyone can change the way they think and feel about their past, their future, and how they live today. While this lifestyle revelation is an intentionally simple concept, it will require you to form good habits while breaking bad ones, which isn't always easy to do.

When you leave your attitude to chance, you truly are gambling on which attitude will make an appearance. Most times odds are not in your favor that the right one will present itself. You need to focus on attitude preparation versus an attitude reaction.

What is attitude preparation? Everyone knows they are going to face certain obstacles in life. Through realizing this and preparing your mind for it, you can make sure you're fueling the right attitude for life's biggest decisions that are impacted by your attitude. You must question everything. When you get to the A-Action chapter, you'll find a great section about Third-Party Action Driving Questions that will help you do this in a more positive, informative, and solutions-based manner.

With questions, you can find the hints that show what you are doing and why. This is good information to know, because shaky attitudes create challenges none of us need. Through preparation and envisioning the outcomes we want, we can turn a sad song into a glad song. At minimum, allowing scenarios to play out ahead of time is beneficial because it offers hope that you'll be more aware of the growth you want and how you want your attitude to serve your life better. Additionally, this helps to eliminate poorer attitude choices from seeping in, which always come at the wrong time, of course.

Need some tips to help you have better attitude preparation? Here are three that are sure to help:

Hint #1: Complaining is draining.

It's been said that spending time complaining about yesterday won't make tomorrow any better. If that's true and there is no constructive reason to complain, then why do so many of us do it? I believe it's a result of choosing to focus on the negative. Consider the number and types of complaints you initiate, witness, or allow yourself to be part of in an average day.

Imagine this scenario...

> You avoid a woman at work because she is so negative. Simply greeting her with "How's your day?" opens a smelly can of worms. She interprets your friendliness as an invitation for her to bemoan the fact that it's Monday again and, at the same time, express her frustration about having "made it through" yet another horrible weekend. Not only that, you made the mistake of accepting her friend request on Facebook. You don't want to hurt her feelings by unfriending her, but her posts are filled with more negativity and complaining. Nothing good happens for this person—ever. All you find is a bad attitude or pleas for sympathy.

None of us know exactly what's going on with someone else, but if we use a bit of empathy we may be able to better understand. However, it's important to recognize the fine line between caring about people and enabling them.

Hint #2: Sometimes the truth hurts.

The years surrounding my divorce were the most painful of my life. During that time, I was very close to my sister. She spent countless hours listening to me groan about, blame, and belittle my ex-husband. She did her best to support me through one bad relationship followed by the next. She offered advice, but I wasn't really interested in hearing anything other than the sound of my own voice regurgitating one complaint after another. I continued down a very dark path, taking one wrong turn after another.

After a while, my sister concluded that my chronic complaining wasn't helping me and was, in fact, hurting her. My sister was the cheerleader in the family, but even someone as upbeat as her had the ability to get worn down–worn out. She offered me the phone number to a counselor at her church, but told me it was up to me whether I called it or not. Her message was clear, however; she would no longer be my enabler.

At the time, I wasn't in the habit of looking for the positive. If I had been, I wouldn't have been so hurt and angry at my sister and we wouldn't have gone almost two years barely speaking to each other. My sister and I became friends again only when I learned to ADAPT[2] my own negativity. It was then that I recognized the positive side, the reality, in what she had done. Refusing to hear me complain repeatedly, clearly addicted to the behavior, forced me to step outside the victim role I'd found comfort in. It took time, but once I stopped complaining about my life and became proactive in doing something about decreasing the negativity in it, things began to look up. Even a *talking Ed* couldn't stop it!

Hint #3: A grateful attitude is called gratitude.

My three children were taught from a very young age to say "please" and "thank you." My middle child is now an adult, but I can still see her sweet little mouth struggling to form the words when she was a toddler after I handed her a sippy cup full of juice. We reminded each of the kids to say thank you to their friends' parents after a sleepover or a ride home from soccer practice. And, of course, we gave thanks on special occasions like Thanksgiving, Christmas, and Easter. We focused our attention on conditioning our kids to speak the right words to show thanks, but is it possible we overlooked the importance of demonstrating to them how to possess an authentic attitude of gratitude?

Being grateful from the inside out is the heart of your attitude. With a grateful heart, you will find yourself feeling less stressed, more alert, more hopeful, and generally more at peace. It's not difficult to find things for which to be grateful. God's blessings are literally everywhere. The challenge is in developing a habit of recognizing and acknowledging His gifts.

Focus on Mindfulness

In a world where positive affirmations are talked about plenty, both in self-help books and in memes across social media, pictures, signs, etcetera, we'd like to challenge you to think about something else that may be more important in your transformative journey into the ADAPT[2] Principle. We're talking about mindfulness.

Do you know what mindfulness is? According to the GGSC, University of California Berkeley[3]:

Mindfulness means maintaining a moment-by-moment awareness of our thoughts, feelings, bodily sensations, and surrounding environment.

While always open to interpretation, the way we view ourselves internally is significant. With affirmations, we are trying to engage our minds to think differently about ourselves in some way. It involves repetition and a very direct effort to master your thinking and create favorable new thought patterns. This is fine, of course, but is it always enough? Here's some interesting insight we found from a Psychology Today[4] article. The article shares:

"The researchers asked people with low self-esteem to say, 'I am a lovable person.' They then measured the participants' moods and their feelings about themselves. The low esteem group felt worse afterwards compared with others who did not. However, people with high self-esteem felt better after repeating the positive affirmation–but only slightly. The psychologists then asked the participants to list negative and positive thoughts about themselves. They found, paradoxically, those with low self-esteem were in a better mood when they were allowed to have negative thoughts than when they were asked to focus exclusively on affirmative thoughts.

The researchers suggest that, like overly positive praise, unreasonably positive self-statements, such as 'I accept myself completely' can provoke contradictory thoughts in individuals with low self-esteem. When positive self-statements strongly conflict with self-perception, the researchers argue, there is not mere resistance but a reinforcing of self-perception. People who view themselves as unlovable, for example, find that saying the opposite of their belief are so unbelievable that it strengthens their own negative view rather than reversing it."

It's hard to imagine how something so good for you could backfire like that, isn't it? The article goes on to explain why and even shows some of the past research that supports that affirmations are not always the answer. However, mindfulness does offer solutions because it involves taking you–as you are–to deal with your environment as it is in the present. Dr. Stephen Hayes is a researcher who has great insight about mindfulness:

> "…what we could call 'Third Wave Psychologists' are focusing less on how to manipulate the content of our thoughts (a focus on cognitive psychotherapy) and more on how to change their context–to modify the way we see thoughts and feelings so they can't control our behavior. Whereas cognitive therapists speak of 'cognitive errors' and 'distorted interpretation,' Hayes and his colleagues encourage mindfulness, the meditation-inspired practice of observing thoughts without getting entangled by them–imagine the thoughts being a leaf or canoe floating down the stream."

Positive thoughts are obviously important to everything we do for a more thoughtful and inspired life. We've shared information that shows the importance of mindfulness throughout this book, along with some mentions of affirmations. The reason for doing this is to give you the options for tools that may work best for you.

One of the most effective ways Kirk and I have achieved mindfulness for the challenges we face and the successes we accomplish is by asking a simple question: *How do I ADAPT² this?* When you ask yourself this question you suddenly have six of the most powerful words in the history of personal development at your immediate disposal. Words that, when used together, force your mind to work toward an effective solution. We don't all find our way to the ADAPT² lifestyle the same way. Learning what works most effectively for you is important. We're the guides for your journey, sharing what's worked for us.

Take a Look at Kirk's #1
A-Attitude Adjusting Formula

There are two types of attitudes: gratitudes and baditudes. Gratitude's are what we strive for, as they are good, positive attitudes with a grateful heart.

Conversely, baditudes are something we should fight against. They destroy performance in the short-term and preclude us from success and happiness in the long-term. Baditudes are bad attitudes. When you recognize a baditude coming on you need to snap out of it as quickly as possible. Try the attitude adjusting formula below to adjust a baditude.

1. Recognize and acknowledge your baditude.
2. Ask yourself, "How do I ADAPT[2] it?"
3. Redirect your thoughts toward a solution for you baditude.
4. Give your baditude an adjustment.

Of course, attitude adjustments are sometimes easier said than done. But because it is so effective, Kirk has found six great ways to help him adjust his attitude when necessary. Perhaps they can work for you, too.

Kirk's Six Little Tips for a Big Change in Attitude

1. When I realize I am experiencing a poor attitude I like to shout internally to myself "BOOYA!" Which means **B**ring **O**ut **O**ptimism in **Y**our **A**ttitude (**BOOYA**). Then I ask myself if my attitude is bringing out optimism at that moment. Can you say it? "BOOYA!" Let your attitude display optimism to the world!

2. What if my attitude is being affected by negative events of the day? I say, "It's just mud" and pull the tear-off, clearing my muddied vision and improving my attitude. This prevents the small events from piling up and having a long-term effect on my attitude.

3. When I feel a bad attitude or what I call a *baditude* coming on, I like to say, "You're only one workout away from a good mood." God has created us with some awesome warriors that fight bad attitudes. They are called endorphins. Put your endorphins to work ASAP to kick the crap out of your poor attitude. Your endorphins love ganging up on your baditude!

4. I love overcoming a poor attitude with American Theologian Reinhold Niebuhr's Serenity Prayer: "God grant me the serenity to accept the things I cannot change, the courage to change the things I can, and the wisdom to know the difference." This wonderful and inspiring message allows me to quickly assess and determine if my attitude is affected by something that is out of my control. If the answer is yes, then I need to ask God for P-Patience. If the answer is no, I ask God to help me make the correct A-Action to improve my attitude.

5. Give your attitude a mini-mind reboot. In the T-Training chapter you will learn about my Tropical Island Reboot. Create a mini-version of this to remind yourself of the importance of a good attitude.

6. If you're experiencing a bad attitude at work, try firing yourself! Firing yourself might be what you need to reignite your passion at work. You will learn more about firing yourself in the T-Trust chapter.

Do you find that you are at war sometimes with your attitude? Hopefully the attitude changing formula I shared will help. This, along with a big assist from God, helps you combat inner rebellions and replace them with inner peace. It's a shift in perspective that you will feel and appreciate.

And Always Know…

Throughout the Bible we are instructed to give thanks and show gratitude.

Rejoice always, pray continually, give thanks in all circumstances; for this is God's will for you in Christ Jesus.
(1 Thessalonians 5:16-18, NIV)

BONUS ONLINE CONTENT: Find additional resources on improving your A-Attitude at www.adapt2principle.com.

CHAPTER 3

ADAPT²: IS D-DISCIPLINE A DIRTY WORD TO YOU?

Ten years ago, I made a commitment to run a 13.1 mile, half marathon with my sister, an idea that stemmed from a challenge made in jest while under the foggy influence of warm cocktails on a cold New Year's Eve. "Linda, let's just do it!" she urged. Before that time, I was much more familiar with a bag of Nacho Flavor Doritos than a pair of Brooks running shoes! Still, I agreed.

We giggled and slapped each other a high-five following our first training run. We would have jumped up and down, too, if we'd had enough breath left in us to do so. It seemed that a mere two-tenths of a mile jaunt had sucked away all but what was necessary to keep us standing upright! "It's a start," we kept saying.

Like United States postal workers, we refused to allow rain, snow, or sleet to keep us from accomplishing our mission. We put the work in and marveled at how our bodies were adapting to the new regimen we had implemented. Two-tenths of a mile soon turned into a full mile; one mile turned into two; two into three; and before we knew it, we had successfully completed our first–and last–half marathon. It was a rewarding experience that took sixteen weeks of training to accomplish.

Both my sister and I agree the whole experience was a positive one. Through a tremendous amount of grit and determination we accomplished what we once thought was impossible. Why then did we hang up our running shoes so soon after reaching our goal? I had enjoyed myself, felt accomplished for doing it, and experienced a real sense of achievement. Yet, I didn't want more of that? Why? Then, I chalked it up to a one-time thing; however, today I know that it was something else. I didn't have a great attitude toward discipline.

At the time, we thought of discipline only in the most obvious, negative way. Discipline was like the mad and intimidating parent, forcing us to do something. That was tough, and discipline meant suffering and agony–not fun. It was something that took the joy out of the goal, making it seem like a necessary evil instead of something positive and beneficial. No wonder we reverted to our old ways shortly after the race! What we failed to understand then was how a lifelong habit of discipline can be exciting, but will never become second nature to you without the proper attitude toward it.

Discipline Hurts So Good

D-Discipline relies on A-Attitude for direction. A bad attitude– or baditude–places all your attention on the pain of discipline and you become paralyzed by the constraints of it. You don't associate it positively. On the other hand, when a positive attitude shines its spotlight on discipline, you are enabled to dig deeper than you ever thought possible to achieve great things for your life! It's been nearly eleven years since my sister and I ran our one and only half marathon. However, earlier this year we dusted off our running shoes and are now committed to participating in a mini in a few months, and to remaining disciplined well after finishing the race. Today, we can evaluate our prior experience and see that we don't want to talk only about *what was* but also *what is to be*. D-Discipline will allow this to take place.

I can honestly reflect on past actions and see how this sense of disappointment had always seeped into my life when I settled for less than that for which I was capable. During these times, things would happen in my life that made me ashamed rather than proud. I'd know, and I'd ignore. Running was easy to put into this category; however, it could no longer be avoided when I saw reality taking place all around me every day. There were often people older than me running full marathons, taking away any of the steam in my weak excuse about being too old. I finally accepted a significant truth—you can do anything you set your mind to with D-Discipline.

Fasten Your Seatbelts and Enjoy the Turbulence: Kirk's Thought Traffic Control

Self-disciplined people tend to have a clear vision of their purpose. And, they refuse to allow anything to interfere with that purpose. They know there will be obstacles and detractors present, but they are confident in the way they've prepared to handle them.

An air traffic controller has a huge responsibility in moving aircraft through the skies. Think of yourself as your mind's air traffic controller. Every day there are all these thoughts flying around our brains. Just like the controller does, your primary concern should be keeping the airways safe. You need to:

- Manage the flow of aircraft into and out of the airport space.
- Guide the airplane pilots during takeoff and landing.
- Monitor everything going on in your territory.

Why is this relevant to a dirty-minded Christian? Thought traffic is like air traffic and being an air traffic controller just happens to be one of the most stressful jobs you can have! Think about it. There are approximately 80,000 flights a day worldwide. Compare that to the average number of thoughts that a person has in a day, which is approximately 50,000. This is a lot of thinking! And, we don't even recognize that a lot of it is going on, but it is all highly influential. The big question is: how does anyone stay in control?

A big difference between air traffic and thought traffic is that on any given day there are more than 15,000 air traffic controllers managing the airways throughout the world. How many people manage all those thoughts each one of us have flying around in our mind space each day? You guessed it, one. With the D-Discipline in the ADAPT[2] Principle we learn that through our discipline we begin to think of ourselves as air traffic controllers for the mind–or thought traffic controllers. As confident professionals, we understand that accomplishing our mission of peace of mind every day requires us to remain prepared for whatever comes into our mind space. Through trial and error, we have learned that our sole responsibility is to recognize the positive and negative thoughts that make their way through our minds. Our strategy should be to allow the right thoughts entry into our mind space and to redirect or even shoot down the wrong thoughts that creep in and affect our mind space. This takes two things:

- Being alert
- Being present (mindfulness)

Like anything in the ADAPT[2] Principle, having the discipline to be a thought traffic controller takes practice. We must become seasoned at this for achieving better things in our life. It can be fun, too! It doesn't have to feel painful or bothersome if you don't allow it to. Allowing the correct thoughts permanent entry and redirecting or destroying the wrong thoughts that enter our mind space is liberating and feels good. Look at the following scenario. It's an example of how you can use your thought traffic controller.

Love is in the air and promises to bring positivity to my A-Attitude. Therefore, as my mind's thought traffic controller I say, "Love Flight 316, you have clearance to land on runway L in my mind port." If the green-eyed monster tries to hijack my love flight, I will use the D-Discipline and take the A-Action empowered to me as my thought traffic controller to have him removed to Jealousy Flight 274, a flight which I know is ill-fated. And, even though P-Patience is a peer I don't always get along with, I know I need him. For that reason, I give Faith Flight 111 clearance to land. I am confident in my T-Training to control my thought traffic, but refuse to allow arrogance to stop me from continuing to learn ways to improve my life. "Pride Flight 2616, please proceed out of my mind space. I have no use for you." When storms threaten the skies and attempt to cause

chaos in my mind port, I call on T-Trust in God to help me remain calm even when everything around me is not. "Peace Flight 1427, I grant you permission to land and remain forever in my mind's hangar where it will forever be protected."

Think about the last challenging situation you had in your life. What was the primary negative emotion you allowed to occupy your mind space? Now think about the question: how do I ADAPT² my environment? Using D-Discipline, begin employing your thought traffic controller to clear away all those negative and destructive emotions. Give them a one-way ticket out, and if they try to sneak back in, show them you're disciplined and resilient enough to send them back again. And again. Eventually, they will give up and not bother you.

Self-discipline is paramount to long-term success in any area of your life. But, it's highly improbable you'll commit to being disciplined in an area of your life without a purpose for it. So, ask yourself a couple questions:

- What am I passionate about?
- Do I have natural ability?

The first question is a prerequisite of achievement. The second is a determinant of where you naturally stand in terms of your mental and/or physical fitness, your work ethic, your personal relationships, or your spiritual health. Please know, achievement is not possible without self-discipline. Your ability to finish what you start depends on your level of discipline, always.

Even if self-discipline is currently a stranger to you, you can make friends with it at any time. And, as is the case with any developing relationship, there likely will be periods of awkwardness as you become more comfortable with one another. Anticipating these roadblocks is crucial in being prepared to remove them before they steer you away from your path.

What is your reason, your deep desire, and your passion? This isn't always an easy question to answer. However, if you look for God's direction the answer will become clear. If you don't currently do this, we encourage you to try it, as building T-Trust in God will allow you a mental freedom and connectedness which are essential to really feeling fulfilled. We talk more about this in the T-Trust chapter. When you experience this, it is quite liberating. Looking for God's direction in having a strong, well-defined purpose is important, and it also provides the kick to keep the D-Discipline you need.

How Linda Discovered Beauty

Remember, the ADAPT² Principle teaches us to look for the beauty in things as they are, which can often feel like an unattractive point of view. A few months after I began living the ADAPT² lifestyle, I dusted off my running shoes to train for a 5K. As I took my first few steps, I felt an old, familiar tightness in my legs. It had been more than a decade since I'd run regularly and age had affected my legs, and now my feet, not to mention my breathing. Starting over…I could think either *ugh* or *awesome.*

Slowly and rather gingerly, I ran a mere half mile that day. I could have adopted a negative attitude and felt disappointment in myself for not continuing to run further. It would have been easier to focus my thoughts on what I hadn't done instead of on the discipline I did exhibit. Afterwards, I knew one thing; I most certainly did not feel like running again and was only able to establish a routine of running several times a week when I decided to ADAPT² discipline and think of it in a more positive way.

Now, I am thankful for the D-Discipline that gives me the strength to put one foot in front of the other. I no longer perceive discipline as a punishment, but rather a blessing which enables me to live the lifestyle I used to think was reserved for other people.

Becoming self-disciplined does not happen overnight; it is learned and practiced. Our minds are first rigid to change before they become willing participants in being kneaded into a disciplined mind. It's uncomfortable and awkward, but only for a while. The transition is highly dependent on your self-talk. That's why it's important to remember your BFF—your A-Attitude.

Charles Duhigg, author of *The Power of Habit*, explains that habit behaviors are traced to a part of the brain called the basal ganglia—a portion of the brain associated with emotions, patterns, and memories. Decisions, on the other hand, are made in the prefrontal cortex, a completely different area. When a behavior becomes habit, we stop using our decision-making skills and instead function on autopilot. Therefore, breaking a bad habit and building a new habit requires us to make active decisions, even when it doesn't feel right to do so. The solution? Embrace the wrong! Acknowledge that it will take a while for your new regime to feel right or good or natural.

The point at which you believe that moving forward is the only option is when your thought traffic controller comes into action. As a trained professional, you understand that to be able to accomplish your mission every day, it is imperative to remain prepared for whatever comes your way. To be at the top of your field you must be disciplined in your mind, your body, and your spirit. It is your sole responsibility to acknowledge the mistakes you make and move on from them; to recognize that it is your choice to either allow your thoughts to enter your mind-space or redirect them or even shoot them down! Just like an actual air traffic controller, your job is extremely mentally challenging and can be stressful. However, as a trained professional you know to shine your light only on the substantial rewards you receive from remaining disciplined, even in times of adversity. The good news is both jobs are highly rewarding. As your mind's thought traffic controller, you understand both good and bad thought-craft will enter your mind's airspace. This is half the battle. Now, it becomes your responsibility to ensure that all your thoughts, both positive and negative ones, are routed to the proper tarmac.

Be an Elite, Disciplined Athlete in Your Life: Linda's Inspiration

Our culture is obsessed with elite athletes. In part, our preoccupation with people like Serena Williams, LeBron James, Michael Phelps, and Simone Biles stems from our reverence for the single-minded and extreme discipline they subject themselves to with the goal of reaching peak performance. Today, these superhumans are our role models and heroes.

But, sometimes discipline and mental toughness isn't as obvious as that exhibited by our superstars. Sometimes we need to look a little deeper to find it. Recently, I discovered self-discipline like I'd never seen before. It came in the unlikely form of a morbidly obese child; a twelve or thirteen-year-old girl who I first noticed about 200 meters into a three-kilometer middle school cross-country race. Her event was the last scheduled for the hundreds of seventh and eighth grade girls entered in the meet. The better fit, more conditioned runners had already competed at the varsity or junior varsity level for which they'd qualified. Even though she was up against the slower competition, it was evident she didn't dare hope for more than just putting one foot in front of the other during the race. It appeared her only goal was to cover the ground and reach the finish line.

Just seconds into the race, it didn't look like that was even a remote possibility. Carrying her ample weight just a couple hundred meters seemed to be all she had to give. Meanwhile, the other middle-schoolers remained tightly in a pack, well on their way to the finish line while this girl was already walking by herself like a lone wolf.

The sky was overcast and the clouds wept, as I suspected each labored step she took just might be the last one she'd manage on the race course that day. Prior to the start of the event, most of the large crowd had gathered around the outskirts of the course to cheer on their family members, friends, or team mates. Most of them looked away as soon as they noticed the misfit among the other runners. All but a handful scattered to other areas of the course as soon as their favorite athlete ran past them.

It was several painstaking minutes before the course led the girl out of sight. By this time, the other girls were already crossing the finish line to the crowd encouraging each one to, "Finish strong!" It had been a long time since I'd seen the girl. I started to wonder if she'd finally given up, or worse, that she'd been publicly humiliated and made to exit the course for fear she'd slow the other runners down. Then I noticed something that made me gasp. A man who I later learned was her coach had made his way just beyond the trees. It was quickly evident he was there to support the weakest link of his team. I couldn't hear what he was saying, but his words strengthened her will and were enough to push her successfully across the finish line!

As I continued to watch the girl and her coach, I couldn't help but think about the ADAPT[2] Principle and how her tenacious spirit and his support demonstrated everything about it. When I struggle to reach my goals now, I think about that girl and how she demonstrated an A-Attitude of optimism and strength. I strive to be as D-Disciplined as she was in successfully crossing the finish line. I face my fears and take A-Action like she did in stepping up to the start line and continuing on when just about everyone around her expected her to quit. When the pay-off doesn't come as quickly as I want, I think about the P-Patience she demonstrated in not only finishing the 3K, but in the patience she will be required to dig deep to keep in her journey to better health. Because of her iron clad will during the cross-country meet, I know I can push my mind and body to new limits through T-Training. And, I think about the T-Trust she had in her coach and pray she knows that anything is possible if she puts her T-Trust in God.

Moral Dilemmas: Kirk's Story of Discipline

Because I am human I make mistakes. However, I also make every attempt to practice what I preach. This means that I follow the ADAPT[2] Principle every day, to the best of my abilities. Some of the ways are obvious to those around me. For example, I'm confident most of them would describe me as a very positive and enthusiastic person. Additionally, I like to think of myself as someone who is disciplined. I'm rarely late for work or appointments, I don't drink too much or eat too much, and I work-out whether I want to or not.

Recently, my D-Discipline was tested when a friend asked me to do something that was against my character. I don't know that we typically think of staying true to ourselves as an example of discipline. But, I'll tell you, it took a tremendous amount of the stuff for me to stay true to my own moral fiber.

My test took place with a friend, a good man by all accounts, who was in a position many of us have been in—he made a mistake and was about to pay the price for it. Rather than face the consequence, he asked me to join him in a lie. You see, he had used his expense account for a purpose other than what it was intended. Apparently, he took another buddy, one he had no business dealings with, to a sports event and expensed it, reporting that I was the client he'd taken. Well, his boss became suspicious about some items on that expense report and began asking for explanations. It was a red flag, and my friend called me to let me know he felt his boss would soon be calling me.

When my friend told me about the little conspiracy he had concocted he was very casual about it, as if it was no big deal. But something about his confession made me sense that there was something more, something stirring deeper than what he was letting me know. He was truly embarrassed by his dishonesty, and scared about having his back up against a wall. Truthfully, I was embarrassed myself. Why did he think I was the kind of man who would participate in his cover-up? Was his way of thinking one in which he thought that friends did this kind of thing for each other? I really didn't know; however, whatever his reason, he unwittingly put me smack dab in the middle of a moral dilemma.

Linda and I really like him and his wife and had made plans to socialize with them in the future. I didn't want to damage our relationship with them because of this situation, but thought I might if I didn't lie for him. Intellectually I knew the right thing to do, but I struggled emotionally. When I realized this, I looked to the ADAPT[2] Principle for guidance.

Despite the conflict, I had only one feasible choice. I called on my D-Discipline to stay true to myself and to God. I knew what He wanted me to do and that we were both on the same page. So, I decided to be honest with my friend and told him I wasn't judging him, but I couldn't participate in the cover-up. To my surprise, my friend humbly admitted he didn't think I would and felt terrible for asking me to do something he knew was against my values. His honesty and my discipline paid off. My friend's boss never called me and our friendship has stayed intact.

From this experience, it may be easy to think one small lie wouldn't have been a big deal for me to just cover up for my friend, to keep him out of hot water. Well, I know from personal experience that dishonesty is like a cancer that spreads quickly. Covering up for my friend would have allowed that cancer to spread and possibly affect my decision-making in the future. Subconsciously, I may end up thinking *he owes me one* and use that as an out to have him lie for me sometime, instead of taking the right A-Action. It's at that very moment that tough tests are given and either passed or failed. If I would have helped in the cover-up, I might have started making dishonesty a habit and part of my moral fiber. What a disservice to those we care about, ourselves, and God.

It's important to remember that we are all vulnerable to destructive habits. It's our D-Discipline to take the oftentimes tougher right A-Action that matter most.

Has a friend or family member ever asked you to do something you knew was wrong?

What did you do?

When faced with difficult choices, remember to ADAPT[2] them. Use D-Discipline to stay true to yourself.

Go Out Today and Be the Rockstar Your Dog Thinks You Are

How many times have you looked at one of your social media accounts today? What would happen if people looked at their goals as often as they looked at these accounts? According to research from Digitaltrends.com[1], people in the US check their Facebook, Twitter, and other social media accounts a staggering seventeen times a day. Let me repeat that–seventeen times a day! That's at least one time every waking hour of the day. Before you default to the perceptions you may have about kids and social media, stop to take in this fact: most social media checkers are adults, with the highest usage observed in those between the ages of twenty-five and fifty-four. Wow!

Now, ponder this question: what if we reviewed our goals at least half as much as we checked on our social media accounts? What would happen? My guess is that this world would be a much different place, and for the better. Think about all the relationships that could be saved, the poor health that could be avoided, and how many children's hearts could be saved from unnecessary heartbreaks from volatile relationships between their parents or the adults they look to for comfort, support, and safety.

The opportunities we are gifted by those around us to be the wonderful example and role model these people (and pets!) already believe us to be is incredible. There are people that look up to us and admire us, wanting our guidance and to follow our lead. So, no pressure, but that's a big deal. I'm a dog lover so something I once heard about them and God caught my attention. (Hmmm, *dog* is *God* spelled backwards... funny!) It's about how dogs look up to people just as we look up to God. Of course, too much should not be read into these things; however, they can serve as important reminders of how the simplest joys can often bring the greatest rewards–if we have the discipline to allow ourselves to look for them and experience them. D-Discipline is a divine word and a joyful word, too.

To ensure that I have been mindful of the discipline necessary for all areas of my life, I use S.M.A.R.T. goals[2], goals which are:

- **Specific**: Goals cannot be vague; they must be rooted in what is important enough to us that we want to achieve it.
- **Meaningful**: When a goal doesn't resonate with you on a deeper level, it is either not the right goal or not truly important to you.
- **Achievable**: It's great to think big and bold; however, you do need to set up goals that are achievable. To do anything less is to do yourself a grave disserve or worse, it can set you up to feel like a failure.
- **Relevant**: Your goals should be relevant, as they are meant to enhance your life. Really, you cannot just say you want to do something and then not to do. A great example of this is bringing the ADAPT[2] Principle into your life.
- **Time bound**: An open-ended goal is not a goal at all. Timelines are necessary for motivation, plans of action, and implementation.

At times, it can be hard to define goals, because the word is so common. And yes, you've heard it in this book quite a bit, too, but we are trying to deliver the message home–to your heart. In the spirit of being focused on S.M.A.R.T. goals I came up with a word that helps keep me on track. It's called *goalization*, and I define it as a goal with muscles.

"Great things originate in the muscles."
~Thomas Edison~

The muscles that make up a goalization are:

1. **Written goals–from thought to paper is important.**
   Imagination and clear visualization come to light when you write down your goals. It's a team effort between you and God.
2. **Using your God-given imagination to create the ultimate goals.**
   We can all dream a bit bigger with God on our side. He's given us these amazing gifts of imagination, perception, and free will to do wonderful things. Through honoring Him, we honor our fullest potential, too.

Prepare your muscles for victory and achievement. It's one of the sweetest rewards of discipline that you can experience.

Strength in Numbers

While the ADAPT[2] Principle was initially developed to serve as a tool for self-sufficiency of the mind, there is strength in numbers.

Even if you don't have a friend or family member to partner with or access to a coach to hold you accountable, you can find role models around you. They're everywhere when you look for them. Here are a few ideas to spark your imagination:

- Join a club or a gym. Get advice from a personal trainer.
- Volunteer for a cause you are passionate about.
- Take your dog to the park.
- Sign up for a class that interests you.
- Connect with members of your church through a small group.
- Get to know your neighbors.
- Consider joining an online forum to help keep you inspired and disciplined.

We all can win the victory over our struggles with self-discipline. The reward and trophy at the end is further developed self-respect. This is the fruit of all discipline and by finding this, a sense of dignity begins to grow within us and we can say "no" to what doesn't serve our mission in life and "yes" to what may be scary, but worth the challenge. Discipline is our backbone to take these experiences and run with them!

So far, we've examined the importance of your attitude. We saw how a positive A-Attitude regarding D-Discipline can give new meaning to the often-dreaded word. In the next chapter, we'll see how A-Action relies on D-Discipline for direction. We'll see how D-Discipline, like fresh air, breathes new life into A-Action which enables you to achieve your goals. We'll see that without action, discipline is just an empty promise.

BONUS ONLINE CONTENT: Read amazing stories about people who've mastered their destiny through D-Discipline at www.adapt2principle.com

CHAPTER 4

ADAPT²: TAKE A-ACTION AND TURN OFF THAT DIRTY MOVIE!

One of my favorite movies of all time is *The Holiday*. In it, Kate Winslet's character, Iris, allows her heart to be repeatedly broken by her narcissistic ex-boyfriend. It's a romantic comedy with a sidebar about taking action to get what you want in life. And when do most people who struggle in relationships of any sort really feel the pain? During the holidays.

Iris realizes her heart will never heal if she doesn't remove herself from the toxic environment she's in. So, she jets off to Los Angeles from her hometown in England where she meets a legendary screenwriter named Arthur. Arthur doesn't understand why Iris is spending the holidays alone. He recognizes her many attributes and explains to her that in the movies there are both leading ladies and best friends. He goes on to point out that she is a leading lady who behaves like the best friend. Grateful yet saddened by Arthur's brutal honesty, Iris bemoans, "You're supposed to be the leading lady in your own life!"

It's Your Life, Starring...You

Are you the main character in your life's movie? Or, has being passive within your life allowed your star power to diminish? This chapter is about taking the action necessary to star in, write, produce, and direct the life you dream about living. It's about A-Action. But first, you'll need to give some thought as to what you envision on your mind's big screen. Dare to dream big! It's your life, after all.

What we want for our life seems like it should be easy to determine, but it isn't always so obvious. Most of us say we want pretty much the same things. Love, health, money, good looks, and strong relationships usually top the list. The answer might seem obvious, but be careful. Everything comes with a price. So, before you answer, also ask, "Am I willing to pay the price to get what I want?" There are times when our hopes and dreams wind up on the cutting room floor; perhaps for a good reason or maybe because we abandon them, finding them to be too much of a challenge to accomplish.

To complicate the matter further, our priorities change throughout life, which throws a kink in our planning, often making it quite difficult. These are the occasions when parts of our script require a rewrite. For example, what I wanted as a teenager changed as a young adult, and then again after I had my first child. And yet again, after my kids were grown and I was middle-aged and divorced. This is okay! If we're not changing, we're not growing. If we're not growing, we're not living. Action is necessary in our lives.

When Kirk was a kid, he aspired to be a professional motocross racer one day. He turned his dream into a reality for a short time. However, as he grew older, perhaps wiser, his *want* changed along with everything else. He recognized how the sport was taking its toll on both his mind and body. The price had gotten too high and he wasn't willing to pay it any longer.

Regardless of our life's stage, the ADAPT[2] Principle teaches us to up our personal star power by taking action in identifying and achieving our goals. In the last chapter of this book, you will have an opportunity to complete a Personal Mission Statement Worksheet to assist with this. This statement will eventually serve as your life's script, as it will become clear to you what it is you want and need and how to take A-Action to achieve your goals.

It's also important to be mindful that not all occasions call for action. There are times when P-Patience serves us better. You learn, acknowledge, grow, and go. The direction you take is a direct result of the efforts you produce.

You are Fully Capable of Having a Great Movie Reel of Life

There is truth in the adage, "The road to hell is paved with good intentions." But, while this short statement serves its purpose in admonishing us for failing to take action to carry out our plans, it does nothing to help us understand why so many of us choose to journey the bumpy path in the first place.

Undermining vices like procrastination, laziness, fear, perfectionism, lack of confidence, and over analysis are like green lights on the road to good intentions. They give us permission to begin the journey, but put up so many obstacles making it so that we seldom complete what we begin. Think about the times when you've had every intention of following through with your plans, but got in your own way. What prevented you from taking action? Maybe your inaction can be attributed to one thing or a combination of several things. Knowing you are the leading man or leading lady in your movie, it's up to you to go through the process of what movies call a character arc, which means, how you grow and go from beginning to end. No character leaves their movie the same as when they started, at least not in a great movie. You are fully capable of having a great movie reel of a life. Utilizing the ADAPT[2] Principle can help you overcome subversive behaviors by using your right A-Attitude to know when to take A-Action and being D-Disciplined in following through. Learn your lines, finesse your role, and watch it all come to life in a most wonderful way, bringing your black and white film into brilliant color. Think of how bright and magical Dorothy's world becomes when she lands in Oz!

Ask yourself, what are your intentions compared to your follow through and actions?

Do You Put the "Pro" in Procrastination?

Procrastination is a profound problem of self-regulation. Procrastinators are responsible for putting off until tomorrow what could have been and should have been done today. This commitment to not doing is inactivity, which results in missing work and personal deadlines. The passivity of this is confusing and frustrating to one's self, as well as those around them.

People are not born with the inability to take action, yet 20 percent of the population lives this maladaptive way of life[1]. So, why would anyone sabotage themselves by refusing to simply get 'er done? There are several reasons:

- **For the thrill of it:** Some people experience a sense of excitement by waiting until the last minute to do something. For them it's a euphoric rush in which they thrive. For example, you are chronically late because you can't seem to get in the car and on your way to an appointment at the time you know you need to leave to be on time. You continue to add new tasks to an already jam-packed list of things to do in the time you've allotted to get ready to go. This intense desire to challenge yourself by taking on trivial pursuits instead of what you should be doing takes over. It's thrilling and stressful all at the same time.

- **Fear of failure, fear of success**: Some people are so concerned about what others think of them that they would rather have them believe they lack effort than ability so they rarely act. An example would be a co-worker who is assigned to work on a project with you, but makes excuse after excuse for not doing his or her fair share. Maybe this person is so in awe of your abilities that he/she is frozen in fear of failure and the resulting opinion you'll have of him/her. Or perhaps the co-worker is a control freak, not able to relinquish any of the tasks to anyone else because of how the results may reflect on them. Either way, this type of behavior is crippling.

- **To decide or not to decide**: Some people put things off because they cannot make a decision. This inability absolves them of responsibility of the outcome of events. Certain decisions in life are more important than others because of their potential impact and understandably require more time and consideration. For example, deciding where your elderly father is going to spend his remaining days is more important than simply choosing what to have for dinner. However, some people have such a hard time making seemingly insignificant decisions, like deciding on what to order off a restaurant's menu. This type of indecisiveness is incredibly frustrating for both the procrastinator and for those around them.

What are your good intentions compared to your actual A-Actions? This is something to ponder, as it impacts how you set forth goals to improve your life.

Linda's Good Intentions

"Perfectionism spells paralysis."
~Winston Churchill~

I used to believe I possessed a quality reserved for a very few, special people. I wore my perfectionism like a badge of honor rather than acknowledging it was something much darker– an action killer. I've wasted hours on tasks that should have only taken me minutes to complete to achieve the impossible–the mythical place known as *perfection*. Being flawless was all consuming, not to mention stressful and bad for my psyche. It's not healthy to feel like anything short of perfection is a failure. Then to abandon what isn't perceived as perfect by the holder (in this case–me), is nothing but a way to take meaningless action.

What is meaningless action? In its simplest term, it is doing for the sake of doing. All that busy work is merely a way to inflate your importance in some way. However, when you're submersed in that state-of-being like I was, you don't see it that way. You see it as being one of those *few, special people.*

My perfectionism negatively affected my household. It used to be so bad it detracted from my quality of life and that of my family. Homes are expected to be a little unkempt with young children, messy husbands, and pets around. Mine rarely was as I spent countless hours doing meaningless chores so that I could live among perfection and portray a perfect image.

I basked in the glory of a kind statement from a friend or family member as they marveled at how my home was always so clean and wondered how I did it. They didn't consider the price my family paid for my unhealthy goal of perfection. Oftentimes when my kids would ask me to play with them, I would make them wait until after I completed a chore. But, one chore turned into another and another and another. Before I knew it, the promise I'd made to join my little ones in five minutes had turned into hours as I strove to perfection one speck of dust at a time.

The ADAPT^2 Principle has helped me temper my perfectionism. I'm still a bit of a neat freak, but my A-Attitude has changed regarding it. I no longer look at it as something reserved for special people. I see it for what it truly is–an A-Action killer. Still, if my surroundings are a mess, my instinct is to tidy up. But, if I have something more important to do, such as spending quality time with people who are important to me, I am D-Disciplined and accept that the mess will be there when I return.

Are you a perfectionist? How has being a perfectionist affected your life and the lives of your loved ones? Do you see perfectionism as a desirable trait or as one you'd like to shed?

Kirk: *Shaking* Things Up and Taking Action!

To kill time during a very long road trip, Linda and I listened to a popular relationship expert on the radio. It didn't take us long to become fully engaged in the personal stories of those who called in, eager to absorb the host's expert advice for their lives. Most callers had very serious issues that they were struggling with, quite at their wit's end for a solution. One caller, however, got our attention over the others, not because of the complexity of his question but because of the obvious answer to it. It became apparent that the advice seeker really didn't need to call into a radio program for help. He had the answer to his problem all along. What he needed was something to help him take action. He needed the ADAPT[2] Principle.

Neither Linda or I can remember the details of that call. However, we do recall the fun we had in making up a scenario to illustrate our point about decision-making and taking action. Here's our version of that radio conversation.

Radio Host: Hi. Welcome to the program. How can I help you?

Caller: I'm a first-time caller, long time listener. I don't know where to turn and I desperately need your help. I am at my wits end!

Radio Host: Ok caller I am here to help you. Calm down and tell me your problem.

Caller: Well, I'm sitting in my car at the drive thru of a fast food restaurant. I want a milkshake. What should I do?

Radio Host: Uh, talk into the speaker and say, "I'd like to order a milkshake, please."

Caller: Oh. Ok. So, what I'm hearing you say is that I should tell the person taking my order that I want a shake.

Radio Host: Yes, caller. That's exactly what I'm telling you to do.

Caller: Got it. Hmmm…That might work…So, what size should I order?

Radio Host: Well, caller, that depends on how thirsty you are. If you're just a little thirsty order the small shake. If you are very thirsty order the large shake.

Caller: Wow! I hadn't considered those factors…I'm going to order the large shake because I'm very thirsty.

Radio Host: Super. Thank you for calling…

Caller: Oh, wait. One more thing. Should I order chocolate or strawberry?

Radio Host: Again, caller. That depends. Which flavor do you prefer?

Caller: Well, I'm allergic to strawberries.

Radio Host: Then order the chocolate!

Caller: But, I really don't like chocolate.

Radio Host: Well then, why don't you go somewhere where they offer other flavors besides strawberry and chocolate?

Caller: You know, doctor, you haven't been helpful at all. Thanks for nothing! CLICK (The caller hangs up)

This scenario is intentionally over-the-top. Exaggeration was used to illustrate several points:

First, like the caller we often know the answer to our own questions and are prepared to take A-Action, but don't. These are the times we should do something and be confident in what it is that we've done. The caller wanted a shake but was so overly analytical about his options that he never did take the action he needed to get what he wanted. He never placed his order for the milkshake.

Has analysis by paralysis ever prevented you from taking A-Action?

Second, there are times when all the facts need to be considered for a wise decision to be made. To do this, you must be up front and honest with yourself and with others about what these considerations are. Imagine what could have happened if the caller, who we learn as an afterthought is allergic to strawberries, had taken the first advice the radio host gave and drank the strawberry shake.

Have you ever neglected to consider all the facts and made a poor decision?

Third, when we look to others for advice, we often blame them when they tell us something we don't want to hear. Don't ask if you aren't willing to at least consider whatever it is they say. When the radio host suggested to the caller he could go somewhere else for a different flavor shake, he became frustrated and hung up because driving to another restaurant would have been an inconvenience for him. Going somewhere else to get what he said he wanted was an A-Action he wasn't willing to take.

Can you think of a time you went to someone for their advice, but ignored it because you didn't like the action they suggested you take, even though you knew it was the right thing to do?

Third-Party Action Driving Questions: How Kirk Keeps It Clean

Back in the 1990s it became popular for Christians to ask themselves *What would Jesus do?* to determine if they were staying true to their moral imperative. Asking WWJD in addition to asking third-party action driving questions are something that I have found to be very effective when evaluating what actions I have taken in the past, as well as what I'd like any future actions to say about me as a Christian man. Third-party action driving questions are a way to hold yourself accountable to what you say you want and what you are willing to do to have it. They are designed to help you take action to be a better you through the use of the ADAPT[2] Principle.

Here are some examples of third-party action driving questions followed by questions you can ask to keep yourself in check:

- What attitude does a man who has a good relationship with his wife have? Do I have the same attitude as he does?
- What action has someone who has been successful in their weight loss goal taken? Am I taking similar action to achieve my weight loss goal?
- What are the actions of an employee who has already achieved the same work/career goals that I have? Am I taking those same actions?
- How does a person who shows gratitude effortlessly make you feel? Am I genuinely grateful for everything every day? Do I truly have an attitude of gratitude?
- What behaviors do an authentic man exhibit? Do I exhibit these same behaviors?
- What does a good woman look like in her behavior? Does my behavior exhibit that of a good woman?
- What do the social media posts of someone with a positive attitude look like? Am I deliberating in my effort to only post things that are positive and uplifting?
- What does the conversation of someone going through tough times sound like? Does my complaining make my tough times worse or do I focus on the action I can take to make things better?
- What action does a man take to be compassionate about another person's problems without enabling them? Am I prepared to be a trusted advisor who offers constructive advice to a friend in need rather than act as a cohort in their misery?
- What are the attitudes and actions people take regarding their spouses as they go through difficult divorces? Could my attitude and actions be the catalyst for change?
- What would a woman do to inspire another woman to manage their attitude during a rough patch in life? Am I willing to share insight and positivity through my own experiences and

reject judgment of others who can perhaps learn from my mistakes?

- What actions do men take who treat women in a respectful way? Do I mirror their examples?

Endless potential to take positive and inspired actions exist through the answers for these questions because there cannot be negative answers. Additionally, through a third-person's perspective, we may be able to determine our areas that need improvement without feeling bad about ourselves. A great rule of thumb is that advice you'd give someone else on how to compassionately treat others should be advice you're willing to heed in your own life.

The next time you are deciding on a course of action you'd like to take that's in conjunction with the spirit and intent of the ADAPT[2] Principle, remember third-party questions. They can move you toward the answers that guide you to positive actions which help you and those you care about.

Our Mind's Final Act

It's tricky sometimes to understand the way our thoughts are processed. The mind is quite resilient which means it is stubborn and doesn't simply flow with the tide in a fluid way that is often necessary to navigate through our toughest moments in life. It's hard to keep up, and when you factor in that our conscious mind programs our subconscious mind as to what it perceives as fact, well, things get even trickier. But the brain is also plastic and through specific efforts, we can begin taking actions which help to adjust our thinking and guide us through our personal and professional growth as our lives unfold on the big screens of our mind.

Here are four steps[2] that can assist you in taking the A-Action for turning your low-definition thinking into acute, crisp high-definition living:

1. **Resist the temptation to give value to both positive and negative ways of thinking at the same time.**

   A great example of this takes place in George Orwell's coined term *doublethink*, which is the phrase used to describe the power that is involved with holding contradicting beliefs in one's mind at the same time—and accepting both. It's kind of like the glass is half full/half empty comparison.

   For me, it was only after I could move past negativity that I could see that positivity had a more beneficial place in my life. I knew it, too, as I began moving from speculating on it to experiencing it. I no longer wanted to have my growth stifled by negativity.

2. **Begin to understand that you are less consistent in all you do when you simultaneously value positive and negative thinking.**

   When Kirk was applying so much effort to gambling, accepting the negativity (failure and the personal problems resulting from it) he justified it by the promise of the big win that would make it all worth it. Only after removing the negative, which really was the entire gambling habit, did the ability to focus on positive uses of the ADAPT Principle (at that time) manifest itself. It's no coincidence this is when meaningful changes began happening in Kirk's life.

3. **Claim it. Know you are going to feel, think, and act positively—consistently.**

   Think of your mind as the *Field of Dreams*; *if you build it, they will come*. Construct a foundation for positive thoughts to guide your life's decisions and desirable outcomes will begin happening. Remember how I resisted the worksheets that Kirk did at first? I just refused to see their value. However, it took minimal time to see the benefits I could reap from them once I tried them for achieving my ADAPT[2] goals.

4. **Don't leave room for negative thinking. Immediately kick out negative thoughts and replace them with positive ones.** Negativity shouldn't live rent-free in your mind. Positivity, however, should be welcomed. Make your mind a shelter for positive thinking and the most amazing actions will begin to unfold in your life. Be mindful that if you currently are (or are wired to be) a negative thinker, this will be decidedly uncomfortable at first. Get comfortable with the uncomfortable—it's worth it!

Should I Call "Action!" or "Cut!"?

As your life's director, it's crucial that you know the difference between positive and negative actions. What actions will bring you closer to setting the scene you've envisioned for your life and what will steer you away from it?

Your mind is connected to every feeling you have and every action you take. Unfortunately, this close-knit relationship doesn't always help you make the right decisions regarding your goals. In fact, the conscious part of your mind sometimes assists you in determining your goals and later stands in the way of you taking action to achieve them. This dualism occurs because the unconscious mind, which holds our life's history, reminds our conscious mind of all the limiting attitudes, behaviors, and perceptions from our past and creates doubt and a lack of confidence. What once seemed like a great idea becomes just another silly dream as your drive and determination are squelched.

Fortunately, with the ADAPT[2] Principle and your commitment to replace negative beliefs from your past with positive thoughts and habits, your subconscious and your conscious mind can work for you rather than against you, enabling you to take action, achieve your goals, and change your life.

A movie producer has many responsibilities; everything from deciding what goes into the script to hiring the film crew. Remembering your role as your life's producer, take A-Action and lead the production of your life's movie. If you aren't happy with what you are seeing on the big screen in your mind, then get back to work! You can't rewrite the past, but you can write the rest of your story any way you choose. If members of your supporting cast don't do their job, fire them and get someone who would happily stand in for them. You can't fool yourself, or sell yourself that your movie is better than what you know it is.

Still nervous about taking on the responsibility of your life's film? Contemplating these questions will help:

- Are my feelings real or imagined? This is one movie that you don't want to be a fantasy film.
- Is the thing that's holding me back a probability or just a possibility? Don't make your story one of a coward, who is fearful and afraid, instead of bold and brave.
- If I take action, what's the worst thing that can happen? The star of a movie is the one that eliminates the danger through action, never running away or turning their back to it.
- Can I live with the worst thing that happens? Our worst-case scenarios are often based in fear that is amped up to make the least desirable outcome feel more probable and certainly very terrifying.

Remember, at the heart of this is your mind. It is connected to every feeling you have and every action you take.

BONUS ONLINE CONTENT: Take action now! Go to www.adapt2principle.com for stories that will inspire you to take the first step toward unstoppable A-Action!

CHAPTER 5

ADA*P*T²: DO YOU FIND P-PATIENCE TO BE THE DIRTIEST WORD OF ALL?

Aristotle was born a long while ago–in 384 BC–and he said, "Faith is bitter, but its fruit is sweet." What does this tell us? It shows how the struggle with patience is nothing new. It has always been a real one for as long as man has needed it–which is always. It's the emotional capacity to what food, water, and shelter is in a physical capacity.

Truthfully, we can make all the attitude changes necessary, adapt discipline to make it happen, and take action. But the gratification isn't immediate. Many times, it requires waiting, which–you've got it–requires P-Patience. A helpful hint that we give ourselves when we fall into the *no patience trap* is reflected through a simple, precise statement in the Bible:

You do not realize now what I am doing,
but later you will understand.
(John 13:7, NIV)

Yes, it can be frustrating, but it's true. We don't always know why we are required to have patience, but when we have it, we can move forward and accomplish great things that make our lives better. When we lack patience, our gears to keep grinding forward get rusty. Think of patience as the lubrication that helps our life run more smoothly.

Do or Don't–What Should I Do?

In an impatient world, society fills our minds with subtle prompts calling us to take action with no consideration of the consequences of that action. Kirk says, "Sometimes the right solution at the wrong time is the wrong solution." Similarly, sometimes the right solution requires action and at other times it requires patience. So, how do you know when to practice patience and when to take action? Ask yourself the following:

- **Are you in control of the situation? If you are not, practice P-Patience.**
  Honking your horn, screaming at the air, and meaningless lane hopping will do nothing to get you out of the traffic jam you find yourself stuck in. In short, you need to ADAPT[2] it. Check your A-Attitude. If it's negative, decide to change it. Exhibit D-Discipline and calm down. Realize you are not in control of the situation and decide against taking A-Action and practice P-Patience instead. Pat yourself on the back. You have T-Trained yourself well by checking your behaviors against ADAPT[2]. T-Trust God always and T-Trust your gut. You know patience is the best solution for the situation you are in.
  One more thing, you are in a traffic jam. This means you have plenty of time. Why not use it to think about all the blessings you are given and thank God for them?
- **If you are frustrated or worried about elements in the future, exercise P-Patience.**

On November 1st do you already feel stressed and worried about not having enough time to get all your Christmas shopping done? Again, ADAPT^2 it! How's your A-Attitude? Be optimistic. You have plenty of time to enjoy purchasing gifts for the people you love. Be D-Disciplined and keep the reason for the season—the celebration of Christ's birth—above the stress of the holiday. Take A-Action and don't wait until the last minute to get your shopping done. Be P-Patient. Your worry is not warranted. You always get the shopping done in time for Christmas morning. T-Train yourself by reading an article about how to avoid stress during the holidays. And, T-Trust that nothing can ruin the spirit of the season because of God's gift to mankind. T-Trust God always.

- **If everyone around you is calm, practice P-Patience.**

Are you the parent no one wants to sit next to at your child's sports event because you are loud and abrasive to the officials, the coaches, other parents, and even to the kids? There's never really a good time to lose control, but in front of children and their parents is especially embarrassing and harmful. What should you do? You guessed it, ADAPT^2 it and be patient. You know your A-Attitude is out of kilter, so change it. Understand that the official might have made a bad call because he is human and not because he's secretly pulling for the opposing team to win. Even though you might want to rage on the coach for benching your child in favor of your nemesis' kid, be D-Disciplined and do nothing. Whether the coach's decision was the right one or not, is irrelevant. Life isn't always fair. Children only grow into mature adults when they are allowed to learn life's lessons. Turn your negative A-Actions into positive ones by only shouting encouragement. Be P-Patient with officials, coaches, and especially the kids. They're all trying. If you recognize a problem you have on the sidelines or somewhere else, educate and T-Train yourself or seek help from a professional. T-Trust God always.

- **Are you always busy and stressed? If so, take A-Action.**
Do you paint a picture of happiness and bliss through social media, but are secretly stressed by the busyness of your life? Do you constantly post photos of your perfect home life and career when the reality is you are about to come unglued? If so, it's time to ADAPT[2] it. Your A-Attitude might appear to be positive on the surface, but you know stress causes you to fight it every day. D-Discipline yourself to stay true to what is best for you and your family. Take A-Action and simplify your life. After all, do you really need to host another dinner party at the end of a crazy work week? Be P-Patient and stick to your guns in pursuing simplicity in your life. T-Train yourself to learn a word you haven't heard come out of your mouth in quite some time—"No!" T-Trust that life filled with less stress is best for you and the people who are most important to you. And, once again, T-Trust God and His plan for you.

- **Is your impatience perceived by others as rudeness? If so, practice P-Patience.**
Does your spouse complain that you never listen? You insist you are listening, but she's learned to recognize the signs of your impatience. As she talks to you about the weekend schedule your eyes dart here, there, and everywhere and your crossed leg rapidly shakes up and down. You even interrupt her and ask what's for dinner as if that's more important than what she is saying. Guess what you can do? ADAPT[2] your impatience. Take the A-Attitude that you are happy your wife keeps the family organized. You owe it to her to take a few minutes to hear what she has planned. Even though you really are hungry and want to know what you're having for dinner, be D-Disciplined and wait until she's finished

talking before you ask. The only A-Action you really need to take in this situation is to thank your wife for taking the time in her day to make sure the weekend runs smoothly. Tell her you appreciate it. Be P-Patient by waiting for your turn to talk and be P-Patient with your wife as she shares all this information with you. T-Train yourself to stop fidgeting. Look your wife (and anyone else you communicate with) in the eyes, and listen. Remain in the present and T-Trust that these small but important steps will make a difference in your relationship with your wife and others. And never forget to T-Trust in God always.

Through P-Patience, we do more than relieve unnecessary anxieties in our own life; we also show those we care about that they are worth that extra minute. What they say matters, and sincerely showing this through our mannerisms and good listening is important.

Linda Says, "Ho! Ho! Hold on and Be Patient!"

Many of my favorite childhood memories stem from those magical days leading up to Christmas. Some of my most nostalgic recollections include the smell of baked goods and pine needles intermingled and lingering in my home during the holidays, the feel of the crisp air that froze my nose and made it run as my family hunted for the perfect Christmas tree, and, of course, unwrapping the presents Santa placed under that perfect, specially selected tree while I slept on Christmas Eve.

The impatience I felt and displayed during those precious moments holds no place in my memory of them today, yet a lack of patience did exist. The reality is that I likely ate more cookie dough than cookies, because I couldn't wait ten minutes for them to bake in the oven. I loved having a fresh Christmas tree, but became bored soon after we started looking for one. And, Christmas morning couldn't come fast enough for me as I lay awake and anticipated what Santa might have brought me. My parents would get so angry at me because I literally woke them every hour on the hour to ask them if it was time to open presents yet!

Age, wisdom, and lessons learned have been good fortunes for me. Today, I'm much more patient now than I was back then. But, patience is not a benefit guaranteed to us as we grow older. Developing patience takes deliberate effort and an understanding of what role patience plays in our overall happiness. Some of the innumerable benefits of patience include:

- **Emotional control which leads to reduced levels of stress**
  Patience allows you to deal with difficult situations with maturity and ease.
- **Better personal relationships**
  Patient people are compassionate and understanding. They take the time to assess and process situations from all points of view which results in better and more fulfilling personal relationships.
- **An appreciation and understanding that the growth process takes time**
  There is great beauty in growth and discovering what exists within you that you previously did not utilize. Patience is one of these things.
- **Better decision making**
  Patient people take the time to see the big picture and weigh the pros and cons within it. Patience allows us to suspend judgment long enough to make informed, deliberate decisions, lessening the likelihood of making big mistakes.

The result of possessing a quality of patience is a calmness reserved not only for a select few, but for anyone willing to develop it within themselves. But here's the quandary: how can you develop patience if it takes patience to develop it? Answer: the ADAPT[2] Principle!

The Lost Virtue

Consider this[1]: according to an AP poll on patience in the US, we know one thing—the US is an impatient nation. The poll says, "We get antsy after five minutes on hold on the phone and refuse to stay on more than fifteen minutes. Twenty-three percent lose their patience if they have to wait in line at a store or office five minutes or less. Fifty percent refuse to return to a business that makes them wait too long." That's a lot of wasted time!

A more calming and productive way to make the most of those wait times (which no one loves by the way), is perhaps to develop P-Patience to productively make it through that moment.

Think of it…

- You made that phone call for a specific reason.
- You went to that store because you had something to buy.

Knowing this, what sorts of things can you do when a demand for patience presents itself during your day? Depending on where I am at that moment, there are a variety of things that I do. Perhaps one would work for you, making *patience time* remain *positively energized*!

- Bring a book to read while you are waiting for an appointment.
- Take a few seconds to just relax your body and mind. Calming yourself down is a gift which often leads to rejuvenation and at times, inspiration. Experience a *Tropical Island Mini-Mind Reboot* (discussed in the T-Training chapter).
- Make a call to a friend that you haven't talked to in a bit.
- Post something positive on social media that inspires your friends.
- Make a new friend.

- Smile and appreciate the rare moment of silence the moment offers you—meditate on what is good in your life.

Really, do whatever it takes to keep you in a positive state of mind. Fighting patience is a waste of time. Saying that you just weren't born with it is a bogus excuse—really. Patience is something developed, not something inherited.

Linda's Plight: I Can't Wait until I Have Patience

Being impatient, and my perfectionism, has affected my life in both little and big ways. I mentioned earlier a few of the little ways Christmas was affected by my childish impatience. Those examples were small and insignificant to my happiness. However, being impatient as an adult has led to some devastating consequences for my life, as well as my children's lives. This is where the problem with impatience goes from being categorized as *little things* to *big deals*.

The years I spent going through the *divorce crazies* I talked about in the A-Attitude chapter were filled with immature, ill-advised decisions, all of which stemmed from my impatience. At a time when I should have been especially slow and thoughtful in how I was going to navigate my new life as a single mother of three, I was quick and scattered in my decision making. I went wherever the wind blew me, just going with the flow. Why? Because it was easier to do that than to be patient and wise and wait for the happiness that had eluded me.

I was impatient with my career as I hopped from job to job, hoping against hope better pay would result in a better life for me and my kids. During my *divorce crazies,* I moved when it would have been wiser to be patient and stay put. Patience would have served me well in relationships, too. Without it, I went from one bad one to another. Overall, I snubbed my nose at patience and was confused by the ramifications of not exhibiting it.

I was not the only one who suffered from the impulsive, thoughtless decisions I made. Being impatient hurt my kids and our relationship as they saw me as the culprit in destroying the happy childhood they once had. At first, I was impatient as I tried to force reconciliation with my children before they were ready. My heart hurt and it wasn't easy, but I eventually learned to apply the ADAPT[2] Principle to the situation with my kids. A-Action worked for me, but did nothing to make my relationship better with my kids because I couldn't force *them* into A-Action. Eventually, I learned the best thing to do was to be P-Patient and T-Trust God that in time they would forgive me. It is with thanks and praise that I tell you He did not let me down.

> **"How poor are they that have not patience! What wound did ever heal but by degrees?"**
> ~ *William Shakespeare~*

Kirk Goes for Olympic Gold at the Baggage Claim

They say that patience is a virtue for controlling your thoughts toward a successful outcome or solution. I fought against that notion for a long time, always being extremely impatient and seldom casual about anything. No time did this quality show itself more than once when I was on an airplane at the end of a flight.

Airports seem to be a gathering ground for the impatient. People have places to go, people to see, timelines to keep, etcetera and so on. And there I sat in seat 22A on a flight headed to Florida, as impatient as the next guy, anxious to abort the plane as quickly as possible. After the airplane landed and came to a stop the captain gave his rudimentary announcement that we'd landed, followed by the current weather report, and then the ping of the seatbelts off sign sounded. You would have thought this was the signal for the start of the Kentucky Derby!

Passengers immediately started jockeying for position. Some of them were very excited about arriving, others looked grumpier than the Christmas Grinch. Meanwhile I, being a seasoned veteran of the airways, had already eyed the *competition* who I suspected would attempt to beat me out of the airplane and down to baggage claim. I paid special attention to a mature businessman right next to me in seat 22B, an elderly woman on the other side of me in 22C, and a 16-year-old skateboard champion in 22D. I had strategically placed my carry-on in the bin overhead. Mine was a masterful plan designed for optimal time efficiency which would allow me to exit the airplane without even a second wasted or a fraction of my patience being tested. I reached up, grabbed my bag, and with one smooth swoop was making my way down the aisle and out the exit door. I was the first one out the gate, the first one to cross the finish line. I estimated my swift and agile move gained me a whole three seconds toward my quest to obtain gold in the sprint to the baggage claim. I had earned my gold medal, meaning I'd be first to retrieve my luggage off the carousel and I was pumped.

I stood alone only briefly and waited for the conveyer belt to come to life. Soon the silver and bronze medalists along with those passengers who failed to medal at all leisurely joined me. In an ironic twist of fate, the last luggage to make an appearance was mine. I had been first in my heat but last in the final race as everyone else had left the airport, luggage in tow before me. Through that experience I learned that patience is about having the discipline to take the right action at the right time.

Linda Asks to See the Signs

We are given signs when we are growing impatient. Strangely enough, we are often impatient about the strangest things. For me, I can be sitting somewhere and talking with someone, laughing and having a great time. But if I see a dirty dish or two, or heaven forbid a crumb on the table, my tendency is to want to go and pick it up. If I don't, I grow distracted, impatient for there to be the right pause in which to do that simple task. It's silly because it doesn't hurt anything, but it is also a sign that I need to put my patience in check.

Other signs indicating impatience include:

- Tightening of the hands and fists
- Clenching your jaw
- Tapping your feet incessantly (and moving your legs up and down)
- Snappiness and irritability at strange moments
- Stress and anxiety

These signs are most always linked to impatience of some sort, and for various reasons. Perhaps you need to invest some time in learning what your personal triggers are in situations where you are teetering on the impatient. Maybe you have a job review coming up and just want it to be over with. Perhaps you are so eager for your vacation that you're struggling to make it through what needs to be done before you to take it. Medical concerns are often a source of impatience for people. Doctors take a long time and unless you're near death, it can often take months to figure out what's going on if you have a problem. You go from referral to referral to yet another referral to a specialist. Waiting, waiting, waiting.

Seven Ways to Create a Patient Mindset

This is something you may not have considered—if you don't like to be stressed out you really should learn to be patient. Impatience creates stress and anxiety in people, either noticeably or on some hidden level. Yet, if we pay attention to our surroundings, we can find valuable lessons about patience in wonderful, unexpected ways; in our case, through our dog, Dash.

A couple of years ago when we welcomed Dash into our home, he was anything but patient. He had the energy of ten puppies. We should have figured out in the breeder's description about him that being the "life of the party" meant his unchained energy was going to try our patience, which it did! Humans require patience for their dogs and often enough, dogs require patience for their humans, too!

One time this was particularly true was when Kirk was making his morning hard boiled eggs. He has them for breakfast almost every morning and always makes an extra one for Dash. Knowing this, Dash patiently sits in front of the stove as the eggs cook. One morning Kirk forgot about the eggs and didn't check on them for twenty minutes. When he entered the kitchen, he was surprised to see Dash still sitting, facing the stove and looking up toward the pot of boiling eggs as patiently as could be. Lesson learned. Dash figured out what many of us still need to learn; that good things really do come to those who wait!

Dash is proof that anyone can learn patience and are much more enjoyable to be around when they exhibit it. It's ironic that our crazy puppy turned into such a sweet and wonderful member of our family, and became a reminder of the importance of patience to us.

We came across this excellent resource list[2] for unconventional methods you can use to develop patience. This list is invaluable, as there is something on it that everyone can either relate to or do.

1. **Read**: Kirk has always embraced reading to keep those lessons in check that help him with his goals, ambitions, and motivation. It makes sense that reading is a great way to develop patience. Reading, in and of itself, requires patience. Think about it. Are you a patient reader or do you flip to the last page of a book because you can't wait to find out what happens at the end of a story?

2. **Shift perspectives**: Changing perspectives means we lessen our risk of having tunnel vision in our lives. And few things test our patience more than everything not going precisely according to *our* plans.

3. **Take the green thumb initiative**: From research done on how growing plants can increase patience[3], we learned this: "The tomatoes we are growing are of the indeterminate variety. This means their growth is 'indeterminate' in the sense that they will grow for as long as you allow them to; they are true vines." So, be P-Patient and enjoy the *fruit* of your labor!

4. **Cook**: Not only is cooking a wonderful way to relax the mind if you do it solo and a great activity to do with those you care about, it's also an excellent way to develop patience. Cooking requires being in the moment and not rushing things. If you do, your food won't turn out the way you want it. Become a master chef of your patience development!

5. **Create**: Many people have taken to the methodical process of creating scrapbooks, homemade greeting cards, and even taking on projects such as painting or writing a book (hint, hint for us). By doing this, you recognize that the effort

you put in is a direct result of what you get out of it. Going quicker doesn't make things better, and you miss the joy of the connectivity to the project.

6. **Plan adventures**: We touched on this a bit. When you take a vacation, it requires you to wait for something. This is the ideal time to appreciate that waiting period, knowing that a beautiful adventure is waiting for you at the end of it. When I went to Hawaii with my mother, it was hard to wait all those months for it to happen, especially since we were going to see my daughter who was stationed there.

7. **Time management**: This is simple. Rushed time is stressed time, which absolutely goes against patience. Remember—time management has nothing to do with urgency; it's about reducing the unnecessary sense of urgency that causes stress in your life.

And if these seven unconventional patience practicing ideas are challenging for you to implement into your life (despite their goodness), try a little humor:

> **"The key to everything is patience.**
> **You get the chicken by hatching the**
> **egg, not by smashing it open."**
> *~Arnold Glasow, American humorist~*

A Parable of Patience

There was a man out on a walk in the park one wonderful spring day and he happened to stumble upon a cocoon. There was a crack in it that was just barely visible so he took a closer look. To his surprise, he saw the wing of a butterfly there, slowly working its way out and preparing for its transition into the world.

It was a beautiful miracle, one that he was not able to avoid watching. So, he took a seat at a nearby bench and just watched. Soon his pleasure of watching turned to frustration. The butterfly was no further along in escaping that cocoon than when he'd started. What was taking so long? Was it in trouble?

He thought, *maybe I should help.*

Doubts began to flood his mind. Was the butterfly in trouble? How long would this take? He wanted to see it, but he had other things to do, which meant sitting there all day was not an option.

Finally fed up with waiting, the man walked up to the struggling butterfly and pulled out his small Swiss Army Knife. Taking out the small scissors attachment, he put a tiny slit into the cocoon to assist the butterfly. This way the beautiful creature would be freed and he'd be on his way.

Only this plan did not work for the butterfly.

Still watching, now a bit horrified, the man looked at the body of the butterfly. Its body was swollen and its wings were small. It was struggling.

He wanted to help so he grabbed the frail butterfly and gently placed it on a patch of green grass.

Then he waited, knowing that he'd finally get to see it take flight.

Only it didn't. Plus, its body was still distorted.

The butterfly began to move around on the ground, disheartening the man further. What he did not know was this: in order for butterflies to take flight, they must first struggle with that small opening. This is how the fluid from the body spreads to the wings so they expand and can take flight.

His lack of patience had ruined the butterfly's process.

Once he realized what had happened, the man understood the importance of patience just a bit more. You see, everyone and everything has struggles at one time or another. Forcing through them quickly doesn't always solve them. There is a process of growth and patience that is required more often than not.

Furthermore, if we were all as strong as we desired, we'd never realize the power of faith in our journey. It means everything. Without it, we become the butterfly that never got its chance to take flight.

Don't grow frustrated with the process and abandon patience, because patience will serve you well. Patience is strength, not weakness.

Practice Your P-Patience in All You Do

When we allow ourselves to transition from thinking of patience as a negative quality, we can begin to shine by using P-Patience principles in everything we do. This is how great things are done, and significant strides in living the ADAPT[2] Principle type of life are made.

And believe us when we tell you, we know it is not always easy. However, it is always worth it.

Mathematically speaking, the shortest distance between two points is a straight line, but that's rarely true when referring to life. Life and the goals we set within it aren't always accomplished along a straight path. Our journey is more like a walk up and over hills and mountains, through peaks and valleys. Success requires P-Patience and the realization that, while the straight line might lead us to our destination more quickly and with fewer frustrations, the highs and lows are necessary for our growth and development.

When you reach a plateau and feel as if you've stopped making progress or even stepped backwards, check your A-Attitude. Realize that the enemy is trying to convince you that your good work is and always will be fruitless. Be positive and understand that plateaus are just part of the journey. Have D-Discipline in fighting through them and keep taking the A-Action necessary to reach your goals. P-Patience will get you through as your T-Training has taught you this. T-Trust yourself, the ADAPT[2] Principle, and, of course, always trust God and remember each step you take He takes with you.

As a parting thought to this, we'd like to share the Footprints poem with you, a beautiful poem that has been traced back to 1936, and has been credited and copyrighted to several sources. It offers a wonderful recollection of the gifts that come through P-Patience.

One night I dreamed a dream.
As I was walking along the beach with my Lord.
Across the dark sky flashed scenes from my life.
For each scene, I noticed two sets of footprints in the sand,
One belonging to me and one to my Lord.

After the last scene of my life flashed before me,
I looked back at the footprints in the sand.
I noticed that at many times along the path of my life,
especially at the very lowest and saddest times,
there was only one set of footprints.

This really troubled me, so I asked the Lord about it.
"Lord, you said once I decided to follow you,
You'd walk with me all the way.
But I noticed that during the saddest and most troublesome times of my life,
there was only one set of footprints.
I don't understand why, when I needed you the most,
you would leave me."

He whispered, "My precious child, I love you and will never leave you
Never, ever, during your trials and testings.
When you saw only one set of footprints,
It was then that I carried you."

BONUS ONLINE CONTENT: Measure your level of patience with the FREE ADAPT2 P-Patience quiz available only at www.adapt2principle.com.

CHAPTER 6

ADAPT²: T-TRAINING TO TIDY UP THE DIRT

It's a war out there, seemingly every day. You have your wife, husband, or significant other telling you that you need to spend more time at home. These important people mention how you never invest in vacations or getaways as a family any longer. You're trying–really you are–but it's only amplified when you get to work and your boss is lecturing you that your production is not where it should be. Your customers are telling you that your prices are too high and if you don't find a way to lower them they will have to replace you. You find out your kids are doing poorly in school. You speak to your daughter and she's telling you that she is so stressed out because of all the peer pressure she is getting from a fellow student.

Everything is happening at once and you're more frustrated than fulfilled. And you can't forget it, because your inner self is screaming at you constantly, distracting you and reminding you of what isn't done, not what you have done. What do you do when all of this becomes too much? The solution is to declare war on those thoughts and learn to ADAPT² them. Like all battles, it takes strategy, training, and implementation to make it work.

A common *go-to* source for training one's mind to become better is the use of personal development books. Kirk has always loved this genre which has been around for centuries, offering people various paths to improvement. Today, the personal development market is a massive one[1]:

> "Few things rally us to the cause of personal growth as the dawning of a new year. It's a prime opportunity to start doing what we should and stop doing what we shouldn't. Americans agree. Our own survey of 300 adults revealed that 86 percent made one or more self-improvement resolutions for 2015."

Furthermore, this same research also shows that, "We asked 300 adults from across the country how much they expect to spend *per month* to fund their 2015 resolutions. We calculated an average monthly expenditure of $226.12 on resolutions that carry a price tag. But is self-improvement spending considered a good cause by those forking out the dollars? We asked them to what extent they agree with the following statement: 'Spending money on personal improvement is money well spent." Decisively, 94 percent agreed. Self-improvement, they said emphatically, is a worthwhile investment."

What is self-improvement, really, but an investment in re-training your body or mind to think and act differently so you can experience betterment in some way?

However…

The problem with a lot of self-help books is they work with theories rather than real life living. Knowledge only goes so far. Most people don't want theories tested in a lab. They want actual improvement that they can apply by implementing and working a simple plan. This is the reason the ADAPT[2] Principle is so effective. Its ability to work stems from training the mind to respond to all that is happening to a person through one simple question: how do I ADAPT[2] this situation? As you begin to think about and answer this question, you train your mind to become ingrained with this positive way of managing, well, everything. This is the heart of T-Training for you and your life.

Kirk Gets Down and Dirty

Long term behavioral change takes determination over a long time. I have bought self-help books and have attended personal development seminars that would pump me up at first. I would finish the book or complete the seminar and would feel like Russell Crowe's character in the movie Gladiator. I was ready and felt like I could conquer the world, only to have those winning feelings be short lived. As you know, life often pushes, pulls, and grabs at your attention, distracting the untrained mind. For me, it was hard to remember and apply thirty pages of detailed notes I took from the last seminar I attended–regardless of the importance of the knowledge imparted during it.

I needed a tool and reminder that was always with me and I could instantly access. It had to be simple to use and needed to be able to be worked on daily–and without taking any extra time out of my already busy days. In my opinion, the mistake of many self-help books is that they operate on the assumption that the person seeking change has the natural drive to make it happen until they successfully change. Most of us can agree that this isn't true, which is part of the very reason why so many books to help people train themselves for success exist. If this book speaks effectively to even a few people, both Linda and I can agree that is a positive thing.

As you begin figuring out what you need to train for in your life, remember this: you can't buy the drive it takes to improve. Personal development is a challenging daily endeavor. Sometimes it is exhilarating and sometimes it feels draining. For example, have you ever set a goal to have a better relationship with your spouse or significant other? One day, having a better relationship is easy and feels like the furthest thing from work. Other days, you wonder what the point is–nothing feels like it's going to help. For me, asking, "How do I ADAPT[2] this situation?" is the answer. It instantly provides the drive I need to make the correct decisions.

Training Is Anything but Basic: Just Ask Linda

After graduating from high school, I made a bold move and joined the Army with the purpose of paying for my college in mind. Truthfully, I was afraid to enlist but believed it was the best option for me at the time. I was still a teenager and didn't know another girl who had done what I was about to do. Still, it seemed like my best choice.

I'd heard how physically challenging basic training was and that perfectionist in me wanted to make sure I minimized how grueling the training would be. I ran and worked out, getting my body into shape. Every edge I could give myself in the way of training and prep work ahead of time was a beneficial one. When I finally stumbled off the bus and arrived at the Fort Jackson *Welcome* Center in South Carolina, I realized something I neglected to train and it was important. What about preparing my mind for this new challenge? In an ironic twist, it had completely slipped my mind!

Of course, I didn't expect the drill sergeants to offer to take my bags for me, but I was ill-prepared for the tongue-lashing they gave me and the other recruits right from the get-go. I guess I assumed–okay, expected–we'd be allowed to kind of ease into our new environment. This was wrong. We were immediately treated like the animals they constantly reminded us we were no better than, all while they verbally prodded us into a straight line. I felt as if my knees would buckle as the biggest, meanest looking drill sergeant stepped so close to me I could feel his hot breath on my face. He whispered, "What's your name, Private?" I wasn't accustomed to shouting my answers to any questions, much less one regarding my name. So, after I softly answered, I succumbed to tears when the drill sergeant quietly and rather crudely warned me to speak up or else... I think I must have blacked out a little at this point because I don't remember what he said he was going to do to me. I'm pretty sure, though, he didn't finish the sentence with "or else I will give you a big hug!"

For the next eight-weeks, I endured the most physically and mentally demanding conditions I could have imagined at the time. I, along with the other lowly recruits, were awakened every morning at four o'clock. Each day began with PT (physical training), which included calisthenics and running. After that, we either marched for miles in full gear out to the shooting range, where we learned to fire M16 rifles, or to another destination to become proficient at skills such as throwing hand grenades or maneuvering through the woods in the middle of the night. We were expected to fill any unregimented time with studying and memorizing every word of the military-related information contained in our SMART books. There was very little down time. Our minds and bodies were always active, always in training.

There were many occasions when you could feel the negative, defeated attitude among the trainees. It permeated the air, but I also noticed how these low periods were ones the drill sergeants responded to differently. It was at these times that they would do or

To say that learning breath control is one of the most important parts of meditation is an understatement as it is the key to the overall experience. It doesn't always seem natural at first, but it's worth the T-Training to master it and give yourself an effective tool for rebooting your mind.

> Now back to my tropical island reboot: Again, I imagine myself seated, overlooking the crystal blue ocean water. I feel the tide gently pushing and pulling at my feet. I take long, deep breaths in through my nose and smell the salty sea air. Inhaling like this allows my chest to rise and my lungs to fill-up like a balloon. At this point, I imagine the tide rushing back out to the sea, taking with it all the pollution from my mind.

> Then the ocean tide slowly comes back into the shore and I allow myself to exhale, the air exiting my chest this time as I breath out through my nose. Once I feel all the air leaving my chest, I draw my diaphragm back toward my spine and make sure that my lungs are completely void of air. It's at this point that my *vacation* begins as this is when I feel the exhilaration of a clean fresh mind!

How long the process takes depends on how much time you have for it and it can be done just about anywhere. Really! Like many of you, I don't always have time in the morning to devote to much more than a shower and a cup of coffee. Fortunately, even a few minutes spent rebooting your mind has benefits. Also, remember that you can reboot your mind any time of the day, not just in the morning. Whenever you are experiencing a stressful situation, allow yourself to quickly escape to your personal paradise and ask yourself, "How do I ADAPT[2] this?"

Kirk's Investment Advice

The core of training is education. Very seldom can we implement new techniques into our lives without a commitment to learning. It was likely a lack of these skills that kept your goals at bay before, and without developing certain skills, your journey to train yourself for the successes you envision will become significantly more challenging.

For me, using my past failures as a source of education and inspiration as I train for new achievements is a smart and effective strategy. Wisdom can be gained from past mistakes. This is the rare time when "hindsight being 20/20" is beneficial. It also fits ideally into everything involving the ADAPT[2] Principle.

One of the greatest things about the entire principle is how you can celebrate your small victories with it, acknowledging what works as you continue training on what did not work. A great way to begin this internal dialogue is to ask these questions:

- Could I have used any other letters to enhance my experience?
- Was the order I achieved this success the best for me?

Commit your answers to memory in your life's script and game plan so you are more readily prepared for any situation that comes your way down the road.

So, how do you bring all of this together in the most logical manner possible? It's easier than you may believe it to be—invest in yourself! When you mention *personal investments,* many people might naturally think you're referring to their financial portfolios. That's understandable, but not everyone can focus on things like stocks, bonds, and mutual funds when managing chaos and more pressing issues demand their attention. However, everyone can participate in the ultimate investment–that of peace of mind. What are you willing to do to gain peace of mind in your life?

Know this… Everyone has the same amount of time in the day. So, what is it that successful people do differently with their time?

They invest it in themselves. We are our greatest assets, and our lives are reflections of our connectivity to our thoughts and reactions, every bit as much as they are to the environment we immerse ourselves in.

How much time do you invest in yourself? Be honest even if it hurts to admit a lackluster truth.

Are you investing in things that energize you or drain you? What would your self-investment portfolio look like? Gains, losses, or no growth at all?

God has made each one of us unique and gifted and he wants each of us to reach our God-given potential. To be respectful and appreciative of this opportunity, we need to ask ourselves, *what can I do today to invest in each one of my purposes?* Be mindful that the investments you make should have a positive impact on you, as well as the people you encounter each day. We are all a potential source of inspiration!

The ultimate training plan will have three components:

1. **Take A-Action**: Experience is wonderful training and to have the experience you must take action.
2. **Get feedback**: Feedback can come from your own reflections, input from others, or a combination of both. Evaluate it without emotion and determine what worked, what didn't work, and what areas you may have left to educate yourself in to become better trained for next time.
3. **Learn from the results**: Take away the good, the bad, and the ugly that has been revealed from your experiences.

These three components are most easily achieved and recognized through making small investments each week in various areas of your life where you feel you can serve a better purpose. One simple way to do this is to Google the ADAPT2 words along with Bible verses. (Example: Attitude Bible Verses, Discipline Bible Verses, etc.) The results will provide you with a plethora of knowledge and motivation.

More specifically, if you feel it's important to work on your A-Attitude, start by reading an article about ways to improve your attitude that week. Really take in the information, knowing that you want a better attitude so the information offered is worth absorbing.

Take a few seconds to ponder, *what's one skill I can develop this week that will greatly benefit me in a specific area or purpose in my life?* Remember, most skills can be learned with a little effort and it doesn't have to cost a penny to train yourself. Now that's a high-return, low-cost investment!

What I'm most aware of in my T-Training is how it relates to my son's life. I do not want to be a spectator in his life. I want to be a participant. And, I'm fully aware that he is always watching me and taking on the qualities that I exhibit (both the positive and less favorable ones). In order to be the best example I can be, one that demonstrates how to handle successes and failures alike, I know I have to invest in myself and you should consider this, too. Let's be real. When was the last time that a kid didn't repeat your mistake just because you told him or her not to? That's not the way it typically works. A-Action is stronger and more effective than words and lectures for most kids. This can be done without being overprotective and not allowing your children their own opportunities to fail, learn, and grow.

Think of this... What are you teaching your children when you become stressed and lose your temper during a traffic jam? Is this how you want them to react the first day they start driving on their own? What are your children learning when you are openly disrespectful to your spouse in front of them? Is this how you want your children to behave in their relationships in the future? By making sure your T-Training program is solid, you can demonstrate the same thing for your children. What a valuable gift to bestow on them—one they may not even knowingly recognize, but can certainly emulate.

Lastly, understand that a good training program, whether it is mental or physical improvement, requires D-Discipline to daily improvement. How do you become effective at using the ADAPT[2] Principle? Like anything you want to master, you practice it until it becomes part of your normal decision-making process.

Kirk's T-Training Regiment

"A real Christian is a person who can give their pet parrot to the town gossip."
~Billy Graham~

We are at our best when we are of service to ourselves and an inspiration to those around us. What greater compliment than for someone to try and emulate what you do? I've found a series of questions that can help you get your T-Training self-talk started. Once you know where to begin, you no longer have a reason not to take A-Action.

The base question is: why would somebody want what I have? Now, fill in the blanks:

- Why would somebody want a relationship with God like the one I have with Him?
- Why would somebody want to have a marriage like the one I have?
- Why would a child respect me as his/her parent?
- Why would somebody value my opinion?
- Why would somebody read my book, *The Dirty-Minded Christian*?
- Why would somebody seek me out for guidance?

These questions can go on forever, of course. Tap into the thoughts of the type of person that you'd like to be. Maybe start with those you admire. Then get to T-Training for it to happen. It's not about achieving perfection; it's about showing that living the best life you can in all circumstances does matter to you.

BONUS ONLINE CONTENT: Boost the effectiveness of your current training program. Visit www.adapt2principle.com for additional ways to strengthen your T-Training.

CHAPTER 7

ADAP*T*²: T-TRUST YOU HAVE THE TOOLS TO CLEAN UP YOUR DIRTY MIND

Living with a sense of inner peace can be a challenge regardless of the circumstances of our lives. For some, true joy and appreciation aren't a given even in the good times as dirty attitudes stemming from past events or unclean thoughts about what the future might hold oftentimes stand in the way. However, inner peace becomes easy to obtain for anyone who truly T-Trusts God—when we, "Let go and let God." There's nothing more reassuring or allows you the security of that belief. It's like the warm blanket that protects you from the cold air; only it's your T-Trust in God protecting your heart, mind, and soul from the bitter storms that inevitably develop in life.

So, does casting our cares on God mean we are magically absolved from the responsibility of achieving our own happiness and inner peace? Can we continue to do things which pile on the dirt in our lives and expect to live peacefully? We believe that through our unbending trust and faith in God and through the mistakes and failures we've experienced, along with facing their consequences have we been able to find the peace we've spent most of our lives searching for. To succeed at this there are a few things we must make concerted efforts to stop doing, including:

- **Clinging to that pressing desire to take inventory of our every fault**
  This is done through recognizing that as humans, we are imperfect, and it's beautiful. To remove the expectation of being perfect liberates us by exposing a greater ability to love ourselves and to clear the pathway to T-Trust in God.
- **Comparing our lives and opportunities with those of others**
  When we focus on what others have and we do not, we miss the opportunities that are meant for us in life–either completely or by passing them by in an unaware state of being. The more we allow ourselves to have faith that we will never be able to strong arm our outcome (usually because of our ego) the more we can focus on what's good for us, which when done from a place of T-Trust in God, is naturally good for our loved ones and others, too.
- **Putting confidence in material possessions and man over the protection and guidance of God**
  Rest assured, we will feel like we fail Him much more than He could ever fail us when we have confidence and faith in His agape. Agape is Ancient Greek for *the highest form of love or charity–the love of God for man and man for God.*
- **Casting blame to others for what is wrong in our life**
  This is done through not allowing man to run your life, but welcoming in your trust and faith in an eternal source of inspiration like what God offers you for helping to run things.
- **Resisting forgiveness**
  To forgive is to take a huge step forward in faith, recognizing that you are not the judge of man. It helps you to block the negativity that allows you to truly love all God's children (of

which you are one), plus experience the power of grace more readily in your own life. Do you not want to be forgiven for that which you've done wrong? Most of us do.

- **Not being at peace with others**
  Through creating peace and not allowing others to control us through negative emotions, we can often find great joy and hope in our darkest hours and times. The example that's commonly referred to for demonstrating this point has to do with losing someone before you were able to clear the air from a dispute or disagreement. Why do most people not make things right with people they've had disagreements with? Because they were thinking with their ego, not their T-Trust in God to protect and guide them.

- **Forcefully showing a non-authentic side**
  When you pretend to be someone you are not, you come off as insincere and not authentic. Those who talk about having strong faith are often a target for this claim of inauthenticity as they will speak in righteous tones, while acting in a non-loving way. This type of hypocrisy weighs down the heart, mind, and soul, creating barriers for our faith and trust in God's ability to guide us.

One of the best lessons that Kirk and I have learned and tried to demonstrate through our actions to our families, friends, and those we meet is to become more self-aware of what our reactions really tell us. For example, most of the time it's not the circumstances of a situation that upset us. What we really are upset about is our not knowing how to respond to the circumstances in a proper way.

No peace = no power or control

When you're at peace you're in a position of power. This often means that you must take A-Action and demonstrate P-Patience to really allow your T-Trust in God to shine through. There is no greater action you can demonstrate than being peaceful and patient in a situation that may be chaotic. This could be a potential fight with your spouse. It may be listening to someone berate you for something you innocently said. In today's world, it may be someone who gives you a social media lashing for sharing a belief or thought you have on your own social media page! Response in the way of retaliation stops the opportunity for a meaningful conversation immediately. Our suggestion–take a few moments to breathe in and pray to God, knowing that you can T-Trust what will take place after that more easily.

A gentle answer turns away wrath, but
a harsh word stirs up anger.
(Proverbs 15:1, NIV)

Through trial and error, we learn all of this, often recognizing what we have learned most is that God doesn't ask any of us to do what we are not capable of ultimately handling. It can be a call to action for T-Training for our T-Trust.

How Linda Managed Betsy's Betrayal

Betsy was my best friend in the fifth grade. We did everything together. We even walked to and from school because we lived near each other. You could always find us playing together at recess, and then hanging out after school. During these times, we shared our deepest secrets, especially during the middle of the night during sleepovers at each other's house. Because of all this, it was only natural that I turned to Betsy when the burden of carrying the knowledge of my parent's divorce alone got to be too much.

None of my friends' parents were divorced and I was scared by what it meant to my family and embarrassed and concerned about the reaction I'd get about it from other people. Betsy wasn't other people, though. She was my best friend and I trusted her. She willingly agreed to keep my secret safe, a promise she kept only for about five minutes after I told her the news at recess. I don't know how many students Betsy directly revealed my secret to that day. I only know the news of my parent's divorce spread like wildfire through the halls of Solon Robinson Elementary School. It's a wonder the smoke alarm didn't sound and the sprinkler system ignite because of it!

Betsy's betrayal is one of the first memories I have of being hurt by someone I trusted, but it certainly isn't the last. I've learned through experience that everyone has the potential to betray trust. While this truth might sound somewhat harsh and concerning, it's important to understand so we can move forward from it and learn to trust ourselves to make wise decisions rather than harden our hearts or withdraw from the world.

Has anyone ever betrayed your trust? How did it make you feel? What was your reaction to it? How did that betrayal affect your future relationships?

Self-Trust 101

Trust in God is vital, and so is having trust in yourself. Some of us enter adulthood better equipped in the self-trust department than others. That's great for them, but what about the rest of us? Can we learn to trust ourselves after years spent doubting the decisions we make? Absolutely! Self-trust is a learnable skill where we consider and rely on our emotional, mental, and physical resources. Here are tips based on the ADAPT[2] Principle to help you gain confidence in your ability to trust yourself:

1. **Check your A-Attitude.**
    Are you allowing your thoughts to be pulled in a negative direction based on past experiences or mean comments from others? If so, find something that helps you stay focused in the moment. In the previous chapter, Kirk talks about how

meditation helps keep him centered and balanced. What can you do to keep grounded? Why not try taking a nature walk, bicycling, or soaking in a hot tub? These moments you give yourself can really help shift your A-Attitude. Keep in mind the importance of preparing your attitude for the obstacles you will face in the future.

2. **D-Discipline yourself to knock-out self-defeating self-talk.**
   If you are delivering an internal smackdown to yourself for not being perfect, cut it out! Rather, replace shame and guilt with the kindness you deserve. Remember, you are one of God's creations and He does not make mistakes. When you talk negatively about yourself, you are criticizing God's good work. Lift yourself up as you lift Him up!

3. **Take A-Action and avoid people you don't trust.**
   You probably didn't have much control of who was in your life as a kid, but as an adult you determine who you want to be there. Here's a simple rule to guide you: if the people around you build you up, keep them in your life; if they constantly tear you down and undermine your success, it's time to part ways.

4. **Be P-Patient with yourself.**
   Mistakes are inherent to the learning process. Expect them and grant yourself patience as you learn to know and trust yourself. Here are some suggestions on how to learn from both big and little mistakes:
   - **Pay attention to your physical reaction to a situation.** If your palms get sweaty or your heart races when faced with something bad, trust those physical signs.
   - **Ask yourself if you are using logic or emotion when making a decision.**
     Chances are good that you allow your heart to rule. It's been said that our emotions determine 80 percent of the decisions we make, which means only 20

percent of decisions are made using practicality and objectivity. That might be okay in some situations, but can be potentially problematic in others. Be aware of the place your responses come from.

- **Once a decision is made, live with it.**
  Even if you didn't make the best choice, seldom to never can it not be fixed after the fact. So, don't beat yourself up about it. Learn and grow, then move on and trust yourself again.

Proverbs 3:5 provides relief by expressing God's invitation to put our faith and trust in Him.

> **Lean on, trust in, and be confident in the Lord**
> **with all your heart and mind and do not rely**
> **on your own insight or understanding.**
> (Proverbs 3:5, AMPC)

Kirk Says, "You're Fired!"

I've only lost one job in my life and it wasn't my boss who fired me. I fired myself, which is something I highly recommend you do if you are in a slump at work. Allow me to explain. Firing yourself is very different than quitting, as you will continue at your same place of employment after you give yourself the boot. When you quit, you give up your job. When you fire yourself, you decide to move forward in the same job with a new and improved A-Attitude.

In my work as a commercial insurance broker, and before I decided to fire myself, I was less than proud of what I did for a living. The way I viewed things at the time was that I was in the business of selling a necessary evil. Nobody loves to buy insurance, but we do so because we just never know when we may need it.

When it comes to businesses, many are required by law to have commercial insurance. Despite this, rarely are clients excited to see me walk in the door. *Not him again!* This type of response is more typical and isn't great for confidence. I'm not exaggerating, either. Quite literally, I have never–not once–in my twenty-five years of being in the business heard a client or prospect scream in excitement about the insurance guy arriving. This weighed me down and for a long while it ended up lowering my opinion of my own career path. It got bad enough for me to question my self-worth and consider exiting a career I had spent more than two decades building.

Are there good reasons to leave your job? Absolutely. But truthfully, I didn't have one. I had these things going for me:

- I was earning a nice income.
- I was afforded a lot of freedom during my day.
- I was working with a wonderful group of professionals.
- I was experiencing respect from my co-workers and clients.

These are great benefits of my career, so what had changed? It was pressing on my mind and I did a lot of soul-searching during that time to determine it. What I eventually realized was I was having a mid-life career crisis of sorts and needed to decide what to do about it.

During this time, I had two things happening in my life:

1. I was a new Christian.
2. I was using the ADAPT Principle for positive things in my life rather than for its negative original purpose of beating the craps table.

I remember asking God for wisdom and direction. This took a tremendous leap of…no, not just faith, but T-Trust. You see, as a Christian, I had faith that God could and would do what He claims. But, I needed to realize too that to truly T-Trust in Him regarding my career (and in other areas of my life), I am also required to do something; I must take A-Action. I realized that T-Trust isn't guaranteed because it is a willful choice, a deliberate act which builds out of the depth of a person's faith. This was brand new territory for me. For the first time in my life I understood how to wholeheartedly put my T-Trust in God to help me with my career outlook.

I listened for God's voice and heard Him tell me to fire myself from my current job and start fresh in it with a new, positive perspective about the importance of what I do for a living. What He said was impactful in its directness:

"Perform your job and do it in a way that glorifies me (God)."

Following God's advice, I looked to the ADAPT[2] Principle (finally embracing T-Trust) and applied it to my career. Through this act of trust, I began to realize how obvious the answer to my dilemma was. Not surprisingly, it was like so many things in life–the answer was right in front of me all along. God wanted me to T-Trust Him completely and experience that doing so would bring me the value and inner peace that I was missing. Because of this, I immediately started seeing my career in a whole new light.

My career purpose wasn't just to sell insurance policies to business owners. My purpose was to protect the dreams of the people I served. This meant protecting the physical assets and people assets that were involved in the business.

Firing myself that day was just what I needed. I found myself in the exciting position of being eager about the first day of starting my *old career.* I wanted to learn and I couldn't wait to get out of bed in the morning to start. You would think that would have been enough to answer my prayers, but there was more to it. God not only helped me appreciate and better serve my existing customers, He also introduced me to a whole new group that He knew I can serve, Pregnancy Care Centers. This enhanced my life in ways I never even imagined. Not only did this opportunity help my career, it helped me grow in my faith and become the Christian man I am today.

Because of God's help, I have a completely different opinion of myself and what I do for a living. I am blessed for the opportunity to see how people's dreams become a reality. I better understand how certain items are manufactured, how hospital and school systems are run and the challenges they face, as well as the unique struggles and triumphs that pregnancy care centers encounter. Seeing how hard they work to protect the sanctity of life is a reminder of how vulnerable people can be in tough situations.

Through hard work and God's grace, I have been able to connect with each one of my clients and their needs. It's a great feeling to be aware of how I positively serve each one of them as well as how lucky I am to be in my current position. I truly believe this may not have taken place if I hadn't *fired* myself and placed my T-Trust in God to lead me along the right career path.

What about you and your career? Is mentally firing yourself something you need to do to reignite the passion and positivity you once had for it? Would *rehiring* yourself allow you to focus on the positive things about your career and help you discover the importance of your service?

I remind myself of my career purpose every day, and a work day doesn't pass by when I don't ponder this question: *am I here to just sell insurance policies or am I here to protect the dreams of the clients I serve?* Once upon a time the answer was "to sell insurance." Today, the answer is very different and has changed everything for the better.

A question for you...

No matter what you do for a living, have you asked what your purpose is in doing your job? For example, if you're a car salesman do you see your purpose as just selling cars or do you see your purpose as helping people arrive at their destinations? If you're an optometrist do you see your purpose as performing eye exams or to help people clearly see the world and the beauty of everything in it? If you are in a management position do you view your purpose as cracking the whip on the employees you manage or is your purpose to lead and empower them to accomplish great things?

Take a minute to re-evaluate the purpose you have in your career:

My career is _____.

I am not here just to _____.

I am here to help people by _____.

See the greatness in everything you do, and understand that you have the potential to further connect people with God and goodness through your every A-Action.

BONUS ONLINE CONTENT: Does your trust in God ebb and flow? Visit www.adapt2principle.com for true stories of why T-Trust in Him should never go out with the tide.

CHAPTER 8

PUT YOUR PRINCIPLE TO THE TEST: HAVE AN INTERVENTION

Ask and it will be given to you; seek and you will find; knock and the door will be opened to you.
(Matthew 7:7, NIV)

You walk into a room and look around. What a surprise to see so many people that you know, some that you've isolated and others that you invite into your life far too often. What's going on? Is it a surprise party, and why? No… it's not a surprise. You quickly find out that it's an intervention.

"Hello, and welcome to your intervention," they all shout happily.

Wow, you think, as you look around and identify all the members in the room.

There's A-Attitude, the most successful sports coach in history. You can feel the energy coming from this guy. Pretty powerful stuff.

And wow, D-Discipline is there. Where did she find time? After all, she works in one of the busiest places in the world–your mind.

And it goes on and on, the award-winning film director, A-Action is there, standing and eager to get the intervention going.

Sitting calmly in the corner, clipboard on lap and a content look upon her face is the doc, P-Patience. Nothing rattles this lady!

Lingering over the top of T-Training's head is a virtual library filled with knowledge and information. He is absorbing and learning from your every move—and the intervention is not even up and running yet.

And the circle they all make together is led by T-Trust, the one being that will never ever give up on you; an encouraging smile on his face and open arms extended.

Finally, you can talk. "What's going on?" you ask, your curiosity quite evident.

"Well, we've all noticed how busy you've been reading through this great book, "The Dirty-Minded Christian," and we are just dying to know what you've learned," A-Action says.

Oh, brother, you think. You take a deep breath and the rusty wheels start turning.

"Hmm, I've learned how to clean up my dirty mind," you say.

They all ask in perfect unison: what have you learned about cleaning up a dirty mind?

"Well, I've learned that if I have a poor attitude that makes everything a lot tougher on me," you say. Also, I now know how important it is to correct my bad attitude as quickly as possible.

"And why is that?" A-Attitude asks, leaning forward to capture your every word.

"Um," you begin, stammering on your words, "because a poor attitude makes you only look at the worst, and affects every part of your life… I guess."

D-Discipline perks up. "That's very interesting. How do you keep your attitude in check once you know that?"

You sigh. What is this? You feel like you're sitting in the witness box on trial, being interrogated by everyone in the room. "Okay, then. Let's see. By having the discipline to know when I'm not in the right frame of mind, it makes it easier to have a better attitude."

"Yes!" A-Action shouts, clapping his hands loudly together. He then looks around and laughs. "Sorry about that. Carry on." A-Action sure lives up to the name!

"Honestly, it's nice to see you all, but I'm not like you. I don't have the time or patience to deal with all this," you confess.

P-Patience says, "Hmm... That's a most interesting comment. Tell me more?"

"I just wasn't born with patience," you say defensively.

"Do you think you can develop it?" P-Patience asks.

You know it's a trick question, just as much as you know that you're kind of stubborn when it comes to the entire patience thing. But they get you thinking. Finally, you just 'fess up. "Yeah, I can develop it."

P-Patience smiles and turns to T-Training, who is already standing up and pacing back and forth, raising his hand over his head to grab the ADAPT^2 Principle guide. "How are you going to do that?" T-Training asks.

You smile and stand up straight like a proud peacock. You've got this and you're set to impress this crowd. "Well, it won't be easy, but I'm going to train for it by acquiring and maintaining the right attitude, gain the discipline to see it through, knowing that it takes non-stop action, applying a bit of patience, and trusting that I can get it done."

"Trust!" T-Trust yells, raising one hand up in the air, index finger pointed to the sky. The other hand is pointing right at his chest. "Who do you trust?" he asks, then winks and adds, "I'm giving you a hint."

Man, that guy is awesome! You can't help but grin and with the utmost confidence you state: "I'm going to trust you, God. I know you've got my back and with your help we are going to accomplish some great things together."

Before you can even blink, confetti and balloons begins to fall from the ceiling and everyone stands up and begins to celebrate, happier than happy can be. "You've got it! You've got it!" they shout.

Then they all stand around you, putting you right in the center of their intervention circle. A-Action walks up to you and puts a pin on your shirt. You look down at it and smile. It reads: Certified Adapt^2 Principle Trainee.

At that moment, your emotions hit you hard. You now realize how powerful your circle of friends is and know they will always be looking out for what's best for you. Now it's up to you to show your respect and put the ADAPT^2 Principle to work in your life.

"What are you going to do to put the ADAPT^2 Principle into full motion in your life?" they all ask.

It feels great to know that you've got this. It's simple, and it all boils down to two big questions.

How do I ADAPT^2 to this situation?

Am I giving my best efforts to master the ADAPT^2 Principle?

Turn the page and learn how to put the ADAPT^2 Principle to work for you.

CHAPTER 9

KIRK'S PERSONAL MISSION STATEMENT

I am blessed to have a career which exposes me to many different types of business organizations. Working with city municipalities and for-profit businesses such as manufacturers and service businesses is educational and rewarding. Equally so is working closely with non-profit businesses that survive through the generous donations of people in the communities they serve. What I have taken note of over the years is that the businesses that take the time to set and define their mission statements are the ones that are most happy and successful.

Experts that study organizations state that those companies that have clear, purpose driven, coherent, and meaningful mission statements attain more success compared to those companies that don't have mission statements at all.

What is a Mission Statement?

A mission statement is a simple, broad way of communicating the main purpose or purposes of an organization. It provides every individual in the organization a sense of direction and a philosophy as to why the company exists in its chosen marketplace. It can be short and sweet—only a few simple words—or longer with several sentences. The heart behind the organization is what is captured, either way.

Here are some examples of powerful mission statements from various organizations, some may be familiar and some with whom I have personal experience:

- **Chick-fil-A**: *To glorify God by being a faithful steward of all that is entrusted to us and to have a positive influence on all who come in contact with Chick-fil-A.*

  I don't know how many of you have ever visited a Chick-fil-A, but when you go in and place your order, you're always greeted with a friendly smile and a simple question, "How may I serve you?" It feels great to know that these people truly want to help you; that it matters to them. Then after your order is taken and you receive it, they smile and leave you with these parting words: "Thank you, it was a pleasure to serve you." Every time I've visited Chick-fil-A, they have accomplished their mission and have had a positive influence on me.

- **Columbus Regional Hospital:** *Improve the health and well-being of the people we serve.*

  In the summer of 2008, this organization endured the most devastating event in its ninety-year history—a disastrous flood that shut down the hospital for more than twenty weeks. The management team and the hospital employees immediately took charge and safely evacuated more than 150 patients as the water made its way to the hospital's foundation. During the time the hospital was down, the management team arranged to continue to provide excellent healthcare for all its patients and miraculously kept all its employees employed during the shutdown. All patients were taken to alternative facilities and it was evident that the management and employees kept true to their mission statement and improved the health of the people they serve under some extremely challenging conditions.

- **Heartbeat International**: *Advancing life-affirming pregnancy help worldwide.*
- **Care Net** is *Acknowledging that every human life begins at conception and is worthy of protection, Care Net offers compassion, hope, and help to anyone considering abortion by presenting them with realistic alternatives and Christ-centered support through our life-affirming network of pregnancy centers, organizations and individuals.*

Every individual who is directly employed by and is an affiliate member of Heartbeat International and Care Net dedicated to the purpose of helping women who face crisis pregnancies. The love and compassion they demonstrate to anyone who crosses their path is beyond anything I have ever experienced in my life. Each of these organizations offer life-giving help and inspiring hope to the people they serve.

- **Community Christian Church of Naperville, IL:** *Helping people find their way back to God.*

I have never visited this church. In fact, it is located more than four hours from where I live. What's the reason I would mention an organization I have never had contact with? I was talking to an executive director of one of the non-profit organizations I work with and he told me about their mission statement and how it guided every one of the members that attended the church. I thought that was a great mission for people to follow. I think a lot of us have had to find our way back to God at some point in our lives; I know I have and Linda has, too.

- **Johnson-Witkemper:** *Do the right thing. Do the best you can all the time. Treat people the way you would like to be treated.*

I'm kind of partial to this mission statement since this is the statement of the company I currently work for. The owners of our organization live by these three statements and, as an employee I feel that my employers have my back and the backs of our clients as well.

I wish I had enough room in this book to list the mission statements of every organization I work with but that would take up another book. Mission statements do a great many things, including providing a framework for thinking and decision-making in an organization, helping to shape the organization's strategy, and providing a checks and balances for the organization. With checks and balances, a never-ending evaluation and improvement process is always in place.

Let's Play a Game: Name That Company

I'm going to share one more mission statement with you, but not reveal to you the company's name. Let's see if you can guess which company I describe.

We treat others as we would like to be treated ourselves...
We do not tolerate abusive or disrespectful treatment.
Ruthlessness, callousness, and arrogance don't belong here.

Any guesses?
No? Let me give you a few hints.
Hint #1: This company was formed in 1985.
Hint #2: In 1995, this company was named "America's most innovative company" by Fortune Magazine.
Hint #3: In 2000, the company stock skyrocketed to an all-time high.
Hint #4: In October of 2001, the legal counsel for this company's accounting firm instructed its auditors to destroy all files with respect to this company—except for basic information.

Hint #5: In December of 2001, the company files for bankruptcy. In January of 2002, the Justice Department launches a criminal investigation.

Hint #6: Later, this company's founder and former CEO was convicted of six counts of fraud and conspiracy and four counts of bank fraud. Prior to sentencing, he died of a heart attack.

Have you already guessed the name of the company? If you said Enron, you are correct.

Obviously, this is an example of where the mission statement and the mindset did not meet. I wonder if the management team understood (or cared) about what being disrespectful, ruthless, and arrogant could lead to.

The Golden Rule is an underlying theme in most every spiritual and self-help book: Treat others as you would like to be treated. Did the management involved in this scandal really want in return what they gave to others? Look at all the employees, stockholders, and vendors affected by the decisions of a few who had a skewed moral compass. If the leadership of Enron would have followed the path laid out by its mission statement, it warrants asking: would Enron have ended up in the same devastating end? I don't think so. Maybe if each one of the criminal executives who was involved in this scandal would have tattooed their mission statement on their foreheads they would have remembered it—at least when they looked in the mirror.

Enron is just one example of why it is so important for an organization to have a well thought out mission statement and what can potentially go wrong when all decisions are not made and followed with that mission statement in mind.

And, the same is true for you and your Personal Mission Statement. Let's move on to Yourself, Inc. You know, that company of which you are the President and CEO. Do you have a mission statement? What does it state? And finally, do you live it?

Mission I'mPossible: Why We Need a Personal Mission Statement

Many organizations have proven that by following their mission statements, they do great things. So, doesn't it only make sense that an individual could experience the same benefits with a mission statement? I say, "Yes!" This is one of the most important things I have done for positive and immediate change to take place in my life.

A personal mission statement provides clarity and gives you a sense of purpose. It defines who you are and how you will live your life. A personal mission statement is no different from a company mission statement. Just like business mission statements, your personal mission statement doesn't have to be long or complicated. Its purpose is to allow you to connect to all the purposes in each area of your life. Through using this powerful tool, it gives you a clear path to follow to make sure you are connected to things which are most important in your life's purpose.

Life is a balancing act of obligations, combined with personal growth and well-being. We are constantly trying to shift to ensure we are leading productive and successful lives, all the while attempting to keep things together internally and within our personal lives.

From what I've witnessed and experienced, I believe our lives can be broken down into six key areas:

1. Family
2. Social/Friends
3. Spiritual
4. Physical/Health
5. Work/Career
6. Financial

If any aspect of our life draws a disproportionate amount of time and energy, another area of our life is shortchanged. This is the start of imbalance. We're thrown off by it, unable to move forward until a balance can be reestablished. Can we survive? Yes. Will we always notice this imbalance? No. However, it does exist. To correct it, we must begin dealing with areas of our lives which take too much energy and put them into perspective. Align them so the energy you have is available for all areas of your life.

For example, let's say you focus all your effort on making money. Your primary purpose in life is to make a million dollars a year. Say that you're fortunate enough to make this annual income but, in fulfilling this purpose you are on the brink of divorce, your kids are complete strangers to you, you have the best friends that money can buy, and your God is in the form of Benjamin Franklin on a $100 bill.

Is this balance? No, it's a singular focus that only accounts for one area of your life for success. Balance occurs when all your purposes are aligned. The best way to help in creating balance and alignment is through the creation and remembrance of your personal mission statement.

Creating a Personal Mission Statement

My Personal Mission Statement is strong and direct. Under each of the six areas of life, I have defined my purpose and goals that all align with my statement. My hope in showing you how I've created mine, is not only to give ideas for your own Personal Mission Statement, but also to inspire you to take A-Action and define the purpose and goals you can set in each of the six major areas of your life, creating balance and true happiness for yourself.

My Personal Mission Statement:

To be a courageous warrior for God

1. Family Purpose:
   - To love my family; to earn respect from each family member; to be a role model for my son and teach him to honor and love God

- Use the ADAPT^2 Principle to achieve this

2. Social/Friends Purpose:
   - To have a positive influence on my friends; avoid actions that are disrespectful and dishonorable
   - Use the ADAPT^2 Principle to achieve this

3. Spiritual Purpose:
   - To be a witness for God through my family and others through my actions rather than my words; to prepare myself for when God calls me to heaven
   - Use the ADAPT^2 Principle to achieve this

4. Physical/Health Purpose:
   - To be in the best shape of my life at age 49
   - Use the ADAPT^2 Principle to achieve this

5. Work/Career Purpose:
   - To protect the assets of my clients; have a positive influence on the employees and vendors I am in contact with every day
   - Use the ADAPT^2 Principle to achieve this

6. Financial Purpose:
   - To contribute to worthy charities that will use the money to share God's love
   - Use the ADAPT^2 Principle to achieve this

From my examples, I hope you can learn what you can do to create meaningful goals in these six areas of your life. The worksheet that follows in this book will help you get started, showing you how to not only create a Personal Mission Statement, but also how to create meaningful goals relevant to you and inspire you to act.

The Personal Mission Statement
Worksheet for the Six Areas of Life

The purpose of the worksheet being shared is simple. It's to help you hone in on each of the six areas of your life and what their purpose is to you. These are the areas that are driven by your Personal Mission Statement, which should be a helpful reminder of your *why* in life. Each area of the worksheet has a focus on ADAPT[2].

Linda and I use this worksheet for all areas of our life, as reminders of what we want to do and to keep our D-Discipline active and engaged. It has worked very well, and we've gone from abandoned dreams and aspirations to accomplishing a great many things. And most importantly, we enjoy our journeys because we better understand them. This evokes incredible positive energy, even for tasks that may not seem like all that much fun.

An example of how this might work comes from my experiences with my Physical/Health Purpose. I mentioned that I wanted to be in the best shape of my life at age 49. This purpose is in alignment with my Personal Mission Statement. To have the energy to be a *courageous warrior for God,* I must be in excellent physical and mental shape. This is a challenge, which is great. However, I know this can be achieved through implementing a thoughtful process based on the ADAPT[2] Principle. So, what happens when I'm 50 based on having had this goal? You got it. To be in the best shape of my life at age 50 and so on. I firmly believe that we can improve as we age if we want to–if we are determined to and if it is truly important to us. This may not be important to others, but it is to me. My reference isn't only about my physical fitness either. It's about being the best man, husband, father, and member of society that I can be.

The best thing about this worksheet is it replaces the urge to act on emotions alone, which can often be detrimental to success. When I began developing plans for my actions through utilizing this worksheet everything became clearer. There were no muddled messages or confusion. I knew my A-Attitude about it, my D-Discipline to do it, the A-Actions I had to take, the necessity of P-Patience, and the importance of T-Training and T-Trust in the purpose itself.

You'll want to find some personally effective ways to ensure that you are staying motivated by creating clever reminders of how you can be on active alert for what you want to achieve. One of my favorite ones that I've implemented involves my Family/Friends Purpose. I visualize my specific purpose for my family members' literally written on their foreheads.

- To love my family
- To earn respect from each family member
- To be a role model for my son and teach him to honor and love God

This is a powerful, wonderful reminder of their value in my life and the value I want to bring to theirs. It's extremely hard for me to be disrespectful to my family members when I visualize those three statements on their foreheads!

Sample of Completed Worksheet from Kirk

To give you an idea of how a completed worksheet may look for you, we wanted to share the one that Kirk did regarding his Physical/Health area of focus. As you can see, it doesn't have to be thorough as much as precise.

My Personal Mission Statement:

Be a courageous warrior for God.

My Area of Focus (circle one):

Family   Social/Friends   Spiritual   Physical/Health   Work/Career   Financial

My Purpose (should align with Personal Mission Statement):
Being in the best physical and mental shape of my life at age 49

A-Attitude: What attitude will I need to overcome the obstacles I will face?
I will have the energy and strength to complete my mission. No matter how tired I get and if I ever feel like quitting, I will always have a special forces state of mind (40 percent left in the tank when physical discomfort tries to deceive me into believing there's nothing left). Give 100 percent effort in my workouts. The kitchen is closed after 9 o'clock at night. Food is fuel to my body. The better the fuel, the better it performs.

D-Discipline: What disciplines must I follow?
Discipline takes goals with muscles, which are goals that incorporate your imagination, your ability to visualize or produce thoughts into recognizable images in your mind, and are based in realization of what success will look and feel like.
1) I will lose 10 pounds in 30 days. Start date: 7-1-2017. Start weight—216. Finish weight—206. 2) I will be a participant in life rather than a spectator. 3) I will be able to compete with my son in a 100-yard dash (and imagine him saying, "Dad, you're fast!"). 4) I will wake up in the morning feeling light on my feet with a ton of energy.

A-Action: What actions must I complete?
Daily actions:
Weight train or cardio. 5 nutritious meals a day (very little processed food). 7 hours of sleep a night. Drink 8 glasses of water. 100 sit-ups a day. Pray for God's help.
Weekly actions:
Limit alcohol intake. Workout 6 times per week. 1 long run of at least 5 miles per week.
Monthly actions:
Lose 10 pounds. 1 nature workout.

Annual actions:
Compete in a triathlon. Compete in a mini-marathon/marathon.

P-Patience: What patience will I need to incorporate into my life?
I understand that I am going to have great workouts and less than great workouts. That it will take hard work and time to get into the best shape of my life. Rome was not built in a day and building your body is no different. Understanding that my weight will yo-yo and I am on God's timing. Realize I am making progress through my actions.

T-Training: What training do I need?
Daily training:
Always ask myself, "How do I ADAPT[2] the day's conditions?"
Read 1 new thing that pertains to better fitness.
Weekly training:
Learn different fitness routines.
Learn different diets.
Monthly training:
1 outdoor training session (Brown County State Park, for example).
Annual training:
Triathlon training
Marathon training

T-Trust: Where is my trust going to be placed?
I trust that God has given me a healthy pair of lungs and strong muscles. Put those gifts to use. I will never take these gifts for granted. I will thank God every day for these gifts and pray that he keeps me safe and healthy as I pursue my purpose.

**In their hearts humans plan their course,
but the Lord establishes their steps.**
(Proverbs 16:9, NIV)

Two tips for completing your worksheets

1. Completing the worksheets is something you should wait to do after you've read the entire book. It will give you guidance on how to really make the most out the experience.
2. I also recommend handwriting these worksheets since when we write by hand we are forced to slow our brains down and really think about actions and strategies more in depth, thereby writing things down with greater personal meaning and purpose. Messy handwriting? No problem, because this is for you, and no one else.

The Worksheet

My Personal Mission Statement:

_____

_____

_____

My Area of Focus (circle one):

Family   Social/   Spiritual   Physical/   Work/   Financial
           Friends   Health   Career

My Purpose (should align with Personal Mission Statement):

_____

_____

_____

A-Attitude: What attitude will I need to overcome the obstacles I will face?

_____

_____

_____

D-Discipline: What disciplines must I follow?

Create goals: put some muscles into your goals by using imagination, visualization, and realization.

_____

_____

_____

A-Action: What actions must I complete?

Daily actions:

_____

_____

_____

Weekly actions:

_____

_____

_____

Monthly actions:

_____

_____

_____

Annual actions:

_____

_____

_____

P-Patience: What patience will I need to incorporate into my life?

_____

_____

_____

T-Training: What training do I need?

Daily training:

_____

_____

_____

Weekly training:

_____

_____

_____

Monthly training:

_____

_____

_____

Annual training:

_____

_____

_____

T-Trust: Where is my trust going to be placed?

_____

_____

_____

_____

_____

By completing six of these worksheets, you have given yourself a complete guideline and starter blueprint to successfully transitioning into The ADAPT² Principle lifestyle. Remember, you can download these sheets free of charge at **www.adapt2principle.com**.

Congratulations!

CHAPTER 10

AS YOU MOVE FORWARD

A message from Kirk and Linda...

It is our greatest hope that we've inspired you in some way with this book. The Dirty-Minded Christian lives in all of us, and the ways to clean it all up lives in us, too. For us, this offers a great message of hope that everyone can grasp. It doesn't matter if you're starting out from a dark place of negativity or if you can see the light, but just need the fuel to go the distance. With the ADAPT² Principle, you can equip yourself to go all the way.

A-Attitude: No one outside of you can develop a winning attitude that leads to a more amazing life. You drive your change vehicle, because it lives within you. No one else has the key to start the ignition aside from you.

D-Discipline: Your discipline can be developed to become a constant energy source for you in pursuit of all the things you may seek in life. This includes both your personal and professional enrichment, better habits that lead to a better lifestyle, financial success, higher self-awareness, and anything else that you seek out.

A-Action: Taking action is the only way that things can be done. This can be the scariest step, but knowing the purpose behind what you do helps. Isn't it amazing how much you've learned about action?

P-Patience: Patience is a virtue for a reason. It's not always easy to practice, but when you embrace it, it can add value to your life's smallest and biggest moments, plus everything in between. You will celebrate what it brings you.

T-Training: Training is a necessary tool for anyone to use if they want to change any aspect of their lives. Things don't just happen and adapt on their own. We must work on it, whether it's how our mind processes things, how our body reacts to our environment, or how we gain personal growth in something we love for the purpose of achieving something exciting.

T-Trust: With trust in God, you have a source of eternal strength to take you the distance. Remain connected to Him and He will serve your life well. This can be tough for some, depending on their beliefs, but for us, trust has been at the heart of our lives' most meaningful changes. So, if you are not there yet, please, don't abandon what's in this book. Use whatever you look to for your inspiration to get you started. When you see and experience how wonderful things can come to be in your life–things that were previously not there–it will become clearer to you and to your entire life.

Kirk's Message of Inspiration for You

May your journey be guided by the new light that the ADAPT[2] Principle is meant to shine down on your pathway. It's warm and inviting and nourishing, helping you to energize when you're tired and remove the dirt when it clouds your choices.

I can do all things through Christ who strengthens me.
(Philippians 4:13, NKJV)

This Bible verse is one that I refer to daily. I know what it feels like to prosper and I know what it feels like to suffer. I have faced times of abundance and times when my faith was put to the test. Through this Bible verse, I have learned how to ADAPT² every situation, good and bad. The context of this verse focuses on my God-given power to endure any circumstance. This verse doesn't guarantee that I will have financial abundance or everlasting physical health. Instead, it's a guarantee to me that if I put my faith and trust in God I will be able to face any challenge that life throws my way. For that I am rich. I have peace of mind and I have wealth in my relationships with my family, friends, and all others I encounter in my daily walk. When I think, *how do I ADAPT² this situation,* I have undeterred faith that I can do all things through Christ who strengthens me. I instantly have peace of mind and I am confident that the right answer will appear.

This is what I wish for you, as well.

Linda's Message of Inspiration for You

Even though I was raised as a Christian, I have committed to memory only a handful of Bible verses, but thought the right one would be a wonderful way to end this book. So, I naturally did what I always do when I need help and asked God for it. Literally, within seconds, He led me to the verse that perfectly describes the transformation that took place within my mind, my heart, and my very soul, allowing me to surrender to Him rather than fight Him like I used to do.

Just as it has worked for me, I believe that you, too, can experience the joy that comes from relinquishing control to God. It's most often then that He reveals to you what you've spent your entire life struggling to figure out. Today, I know who I am and what my purpose is here in this life. It's good and pleasant and perfect...and the entire journey has been (and is) worth it.

> **Don't copy the behavior and customs of this world, but let God transform you into a new person by changing the way you think. Then you will learn to know God's will for you, which is good and pleasing and perfect.**
> (Romans 12:2, NLT)

BONUS ONLINE CONTENT: Still think you have a dirty mind? Check out the FREE Dirty Mind Detector available at www.adapt2principle.com and find out!

END NOTES

Introduction

[1] Dvorsky, *Managing your 50,000 daily thoughts*

Chapter Two

[1] Williams, *Are We Hardwired to Be Positive or Negative?*
[2] Lally, Phillipa *et al.*, *How habits are formed: Modelling habit formation in the real world*
[3] Greater Good Science Center at UC Berkeley, *What is mindfulness?*
[4] Williams, *Why Don't My Positive Affirmations Work? Affirmations can actually be counterproductive and are not magic.*

Chapter Three

[1] Chang, *Americans spend an alarming amount of time checking social media on their phones.*
[2] Wanderlust Worker, *Setting S.M.A.R.T.E.R. Goals: 7 Steps to Achieving Any Goal*

Chapter Four

[1] Estroff, Marano, *Procrastination: Ten Things to Know*
[2] Fonvielle, *How to Rewire Your Brain to Think Positive*

Chapter Five

1   Sermon Central Staff, *Patience: A Lost Virtue An Ap Poll Finds The U.s.*
2   Ursillo, *7 Unconventional Ways to Develop Patience*
3   Kenny, *The Importance of Research and Patience*

Chapter Six

1   Medenwald, *The Business of Self-Improvement: What Americans are Buying in 2015.*
2   Clarke et al., *Trends in the use of complementary health approaches among adults: United States, 2002-2012*

BIBLIOGRAPHY

Introduction

1. Dvorsky, George, Managing your 50,000 daily thoughts, *Sentient Developments*, March 19, 2007, http://www.sentient developments.com2007/03/imagining-your-50000-daily-thoughts.html.

Chapter Two

1. Williams, Ray, Are We Hardwired to Be Positive or Negative?, *Wired for Success*, Psychology Today, June 30, 2014, https://www.psychologytoday.com/blog/wired-success/201406/are-we-hardwired-be-positive-or-negative.
2. Lally, Phillipa *et* al., 2010, How habits are formed: Modelling habit formation in the real world, *European Journal of Social Psychology*, Volume 40, Issue 6, October 2010, Pages 998-1009.
3. Greater Good Science Center at UC Berkeley, What is mindfulness?, *Mindfulness | Defined*, Greater Good Magazine, https://greatergood.berkeley.edu/mindfulness/definition.
4. Williams, Ray, Why Don't My Positive Affirmations Work? Affirmations can actually be counterproductive and are not magic., *Wired for Success*, Psychology Today, October 14, 2012, https://www.psychologytoday.com/blog/

wired-success/201210/why-dont-my-positive-affirmations-work.

Chapter Three

1. Chang, Lulu, Americans spend an alarming amount of time checking social media on their phones., Digital Trends, June 13, 2015, http://www.digitaltrends.com/mobile/informate-report-social-media-smartphone-use/#ixzz4RhfFoDOF.
2. Wanderlust Worker, Setting S.M.A.R.T.E.R. Goals: 7 Steps to Achieving Any Goal, Wanderlust Worker, 2016, https://www.wanderlustworker.com/setting-s-m-a-r-t-e-r-goals-7-steps-to-achieving-any-goal/.

Chapter Four

1. Estroff, Marano, Haram, Procrastination: Ten Things to Know, Psychology Today, August 23, 2003 (Updated June 9, 2016), https://www.psychologytoday.com/articles/200308/procrastination-ten-things-know.
2. Fonvielle, Dave, How to Rewire Your Brain to Think Positive, *Positive Thinking Course*, Always Greater, Section 2, Lesson 5:3, 2014, http://www.alwaysgreater.com/achievements/how-to-reprogram-your-mind-to-think-positive.

Chapter Five

1. Sermon Central Staff, Patience: A Lost Virtue An Ap Poll Finds The U.s., Sermon Central, 2007, AP Survey Dated May 29, 2016, https://www.sermoncentral.com/illustrations/sermon-illustration-sermoncentral-staff-statistics-31152#.
2. Ursillo, Dave, 7 Unconventional Ways to Develop Patience, Dave Ursillo,https://www.daveursillo.com/7-unconventional-ways-to-develop-patience/.

3. Kenny, Daniel, The Importance of Research and Patience, IWU Peace Garden, June 18, 2012, https://blogs.iwu.edu/iwupeacegarden/2012/06/18/the-importance-of-research-and-patience/.

Chapter Six

1. Medenwald, Chris, Ph.D., The Business of Self-Improvement: What Americans are Buying in 2015, *Endcaps & Insights | Intel on the Ever-Changing World of Retail*, Field Agent, January 21, 2015, http://blog.fieldagent.net/the-business-of-self-improvement-popular-purchases-for-2015.
2. Clarke, TC, *et al.*, Trends in the use of complementary health approaches among adults: United States, 2002-2012, 2015, National health statistics reports; no 79. Hyattsville, MD: National Center for Health Statistics.

MEET "THE ADAPT² CREW": KIRK AND LINDA THOMAS

About Kirk Thomas

Kirk is not only the founder of the ADAPT² Principle; he is a successful business advisor to all types of organizations, including hospitals, school systems, doctors' offices, manufacturers, and various nonprofit organizations. He has developed a nationwide program for Pregnancy Care Centers and specializes in protecting the dreams and physical assets of the organizations he serves. Kirk's accomplishments include:

Being a nationally ranked amateur athlete in his youth

Graduating with a Business Degree from Ball State University

Multiple selections to Presidents Council from previous employer

Seven-time winner of the Producer of the Year Award with his current employer

Dedicated husband and proud father of a teenage son

Kirk's hope is that the ADAPT[2] Principle offers solutions to both little and big challenges we all face in life at different times.

About Linda Thomas

Linda Thomas has more than a decade's worth of experience in advertising sales. She also holds a Bachelor of Science Degree from Ball State University, earning it in just two-and-a-half years. Prior

to obtaining her degree, Linda served in the U.S. Army where she was an award-winning radio and television broadcaster. When her children were young, Linda set aside her career aspirations and was a stay-at-home mom to her three children. But, the entire time she had a secret passion she wanted to fulfill-that of being a writer. With *The Dirty-Minded Christian: How to Clean Up Your Thoughts with the ADAPT² Principle*, her dream has seen itself to fruition.

CONTACT KIRK AND
LINDA THOMAS

www.adapt2principle.com
Kirk@adapt2principle.com
Linda@adapt2principle.com

Printed in the United States
By Bookmasters